SMALL FEET, BIG LAND

SMALL FEET,
BIG LAND

Adventure, Home, *and* Family *on the* Edge *of* Alaska

ERIN MCKITTRICK

MOUNTAINEERS
BOOKS

Mountaineers Books is the publishing division of
The Mountaineers, an organization founded in 1906 and
dedicated to the exploration, preservation, and enjoyment
of outdoor and wilderness areas.

MOUNTAINEERS 1001 SW Klickitat Way, Suite 201, Seattle, WA 98134
BOOKS 800.553.4453, www.mountaineersbooks.org

Printed in the United States of America

Distributed in the United Kingdom by Cordee, www.cordee.co.uk

16 15 14 13   1 2 3 4 5

Copy Editor: Amy Smith Bell
Design and Layout: Jane Jeszeck, www.jigsawseattle.com
Cartographer: Bretwood Higman
Photographers: Erin McKittrick and Bretwood Higman
Cover photograph: *Erin and Katmai walk the rubble-covered expanse of Malaspina Glacier
  while Lituya sleeps on Erin's chest, Mount St. Elias in the background.*
Dedication photograph: *Lituya, near the Samovar Hills area*
Frontispiece: *Malaspina Lake*

Library of Congress Cataloging-in-Publication Data on file

ISBN (paperback): 978-1-59485-736-2
ISBN (ebook): 978-1-59485-737-9

For Katmai and Lituya

Contents

PART III. THE VILLAGE

PART IV. LIFE ON ICE

Acknowledgments

I'D LIKE TO THANK my family and Hig's, for bringing us out into the woods when we were tiny, and supporting every crazy adventure we've dreamed up as adults. The people of Beluga, Point Hope, Kivalina, Noatak, and Yakutat, for opening their lives and sharing their ideas. The pilots who carried us safely to and from each adventure. The friends, family, and editors who helped me work these stories into better words. And our fellow Seldovians, who make this place such a wonderful home.

PROLOGUE
Adventurers Born

ADVENTURE IS OFTEN SEEN as the province of the young—something to do when you're fit, broke, inexperienced, and lacking other commitments. A dozen years ago, Hig (then my boyfriend) and I fit the bill perfectly. So in the summer after I graduated from college we took off on an 830-mile trek through the wilderness of the Alaska Peninsula.

Our expensive mountaineering rainpants leaked in the first rain. Our inexpensive rafts had holes after the first river crossing. Our sleeping bag was too heavy. Our tarp was too small. Our food calculations were laughably low. And somehow, although every one of those things mattered, none of them mattered enough. Poring over the map in the evenings, we counted each one of those 830 miles, measuring success in numbers that impressed us. Walking across the tundra in the blowing rain, I imagined myself an intrepid explorer. I felt proud. I felt alive. And I knew that something in my life had irreversibly changed.

After the trek, we flew south. To the urban streets of Seattle, to the graduate schools we'd promised to attend—Hig in geology and me in molecular biology. But we never really left Alaska. I papered my desk with images of glaciers and tundra, daydreaming between experiments. I built

Katmai peers over Erin's shoulder as she hikes the ridges of Cape Lisburne.

the years around excuses—a honeymoon, a leave of absence—squeezing out a month or two to fly back north into the woods, decorating the map of Alaska with meandering human-powered lines.

"Why?"

It was the question I got from my professors and my fellow graduate students. It was what we heard each time we stumbled into a far-flung Alaskan village, tired, hungry, and wet. Sometimes, I feel like I've spent a decade answering "Why?" Even after hundreds of tries, my explanations rarely get close to touching the true heart of our inexplicable passion.

Because we are here to discover the world. Because we believe there are things to learn by walking. And because I can't imagine a different way to be.

I've never been much of an athlete, and our journeys strive for no records. We are not the fastest, highest, farthest, or longest. We are first in some things only because we choose paths that others have not. We learn. We explore.

Does the world still have a place for explorers? We can walk into the wilderness with carefully constructed topographic maps, with GPS location devices, with satellite phones and emergency locator beacons, and high-tech modern gear. It is no longer possible to find a mountain or a bay that's new to the world. More than ten thousand years ago, ancient Siberians set foot in an Alaska brand new to humanity, discovering those mountains and bays and the strange creatures that inhabited them. Since then, explorers have simply learned things for themselves, touched them and smelled them and felt them, and spread their own truth to anyone who'd listen.

The first things Hig and I learned were eminently practical. Estimating food for a months-long trek is not the same as for a weeklong jaunt. There's only so much peanut butter you can stand. All raingear leaks. Camp away from the bears.

I learned to squint at a topographic map and see the real mountains. I learned to judge the height of ocean waves, the speed of a river, and the strength of a snow bridge. I learned that humans have poor memories for physical discomfort—and that no matter how many times I feel cold and wet, I will always yearn to head out again.

I learned to see the world at human speed. Sometimes we see wildlife. More often we follow their trails—learning their habits through tracks and sign. We discover new plants, then watch where they grow—glimpses into climate and history beyond the momentary weather. We've untwisted the origins of mountains and rivers, and followed the footprints of climate change. We've walked through bustling cities and remote national parks. We've scrambled over logging slash in fresh clearcuts. We've walked beneath helicopters exploring future mines.

And we've met people. In tiny villages and remote homesteads, on fishing boats and highways. With every conversation, we learn something. About the politics of hunting and fishing, the interaction between parks and villages, the promise of jobs and the threat of pollution. About generosity, hospitality, and home.

Six years after that first journey, Hig and I had accumulated three thousand miles of wilderness wanderings, fourteen thousand miles of plane travel between Seattle and Alaska, and two advanced degrees. Then we stopped fitting expeditions into our life—and turned our life into an expedition. With the final signatures that marked Hig as a PhD, we gave away most of our possessions, left our ragged apartment in Seattle's University District, and began a long walk to Alaska. We became the "people who were walking to the Aleutian Islands." And as those thousands of miles receded behind us, we became instead the "people who walked from Seattle."

Summer gave way to the storms of fall, and the long snow of an Alaskan winter. Roads gave way to wilderness. Trees gave way to tundra. Eventually spring returned, wiping away the last traces of our abandoned lives.

At the end of that yearlong journey, we found home: a 450-square-foot yurt in the small village of Seldovia, on the Kenai Peninsula in Southcentral Alaska. Home was a garden full of broccoli and kale, a freezer full of salmon, a yard full of berries, and a crackling woodstove. Home was the letters slowly wearing off the keys on my laptop. Home was friends that showed up to help us get started, with tools, fish, and firewood. Home was

Hig's mother just a shout away. Home was the unborn child growing inside me. Home was a life with the space to make what we wanted of it. But what did we want? I was quickly falling in love with Seldovia. But having a home added a new tension to our lives—questions and trade-offs that never bothered my younger self.

Were we settling down? Or were we still adventurers? Trying to live lightly on our own small chunk of land, I worked to learn gardening and fishing, as I struggled to meet the demands of first one, then two small children. But after the kids fell asleep, our conversations drifted.

"What if we went back to the Arctic?" I mused.

"So many adventurers trek the Brooks Range," Hig replied. "But the western Arctic? Almost no one goes there. And there are so many things going on—those big coal deposits, coastal erosion, offshore drilling. . . ."

"Villages too—enough of them to make resupplies practical, and I'd love to see them. And those cliffs at Cape Lisburne. . . ."

We peered at the greens and browns of Google Earth images, dreaming of glaciers, rivers, and fjords. We wondered about coal mining plans across Cook Inlet. We filled our freezer with berries. We traced lines on the map.

The inspiration that had drawn me to Seldovia connected me to the rest of Alaska as well. The issues that impacted remote mine prospects and Arctic villages stretched their fingers to our own home. My newfound roots and long habit of adventure were inextricably linked. So we built the best life we could in a yurt at the edge of our own patch of wilderness. And with children in tow, we set out to explore our larger wild home—the state of Alaska. We made plans to journey the coast of the Arctic Ocean, penciling in visits to villages and mines, while dreaming up an even more audacious family journey: living for two months on the crumbling edge of North America's largest tidewater glacier.

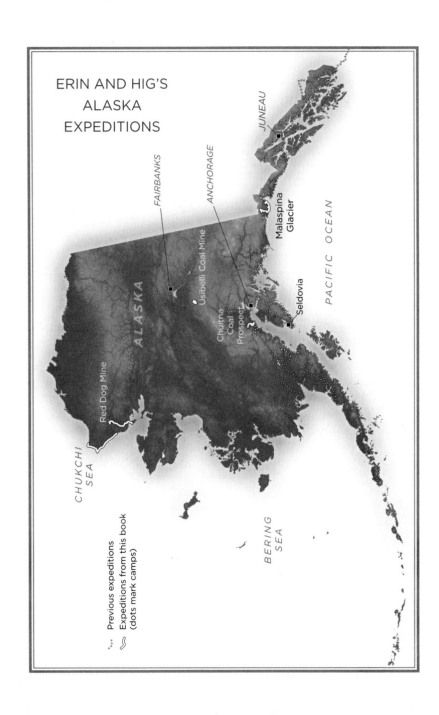

ERIN AND HIG'S
ALASKA
EXPEDITIONS

JUNEAU

FAIRBANKS

ANCHORAGE

Malaspina
Glacier

Usibelli Coal Mine

PACIFIC OCEAN

ALASKA

Chuitna
Coal
Prospect

Seldovia

Red Dog Mine

CHUKCHI
SEA

BERING
SEA

Previous expeditions
Expeditions from this book
(dots mark camps)

PART I

Launching and Landing

1. Baby Steps

I KNEW HOW TO PLAN routes through a complicated landscape of cliffs, water, and brush. I knew how to set up shelter in a blizzard, and start a fire in the pouring rain—reaching for dry wood deep beneath spruce trees or cutting into the center of a cedar driftwood log. I knew how to pare our backpacking gear down to a fine-tuned minimalism. But I knew nothing about babies.

Wilderness expeditions were woven so tightly into the fabric of our lives that I couldn't imagine giving them up. Yet I couldn't imagine having an infant along either. The impending arrival of our son presented an obstacle that seemed far more formidable than any ice-choked bay or miles-long bushwhack.

"I don't know if you could take a baby bushwhacking," I considered. "Unless you built some kind of shield to protect their face from branches."

"There wouldn't be any point taking the baby along on something the baby wouldn't appreciate anyway," Hig replied.

As my due date approached, we continued our ignorant speculations. Before I ever saw our child, I was already wondering how to get some time without him.

Katmai enjoys the ride as Hig glissades down a scree slope near Tutka Bay.

"How long do babies nurse?" Hig asked.

"I don't know. I doubt we could leave him the first summer—he'll only be six months old."

"Maybe the next summer?" he offered.

"We can do shorter trips. Maybe leave him with Grandma for a week or two?"

Then our plans met reality—in the form of a seven-pound-four-ounce baby boy with an elfin face and a wicked cone head. Clutching the tiny shape of my newborn to my chest, I no longer fantasized about hiking adventures with grandmother babysitters. I couldn't possibly leave him behind. I didn't *want* to leave him behind. At home, I sat by our woodstove, nursing my baby, gazing at his sweetly sleeping form, and snapping pictures of every tiny flutter of expression.

And growing more and more restless with each day. I dug through my drawer of hand-me-down baby supplies for the smallest, warmest clothes I could find. We were all going to have to get outside again. Together.

⌒⌒

At three weeks old, Katmai's cry was a high, shrill squeal, his face scrunched pink in indignation where it peeked above my half-zipped winter coat. It sent my new-mom brain into a frenzied flurry of activity. I pulled a Therm-a-Rest from my small day pack, plopped down unceremoniously with snowshoes still dangling from my feet, and extricated the baby as Hig threw a down quilt over the pair of us. Katmai started nursing immediately.

The awkward diaper change by unpracticed parents in twenty-degree weather went a little less smoothly. Still unused to the dramatic fervor with which babies voice their every desire, I winced at each cry, fumbling in my haste. After a minute of walking, all was forgiven. We continued for another couple of hours, repeating the nursing break once more—slowly building a new rhythm to our lives.

"See the snow?" I whispered. "I know you've never seen anything else, but someday things will be green here." At three weeks old, Katmai probably saw little more than a monochrome blur of white ground and black branches. He probably saw it as entirely unimportant—the world beyond mom irrelevant to an infant's brain. My words trailed off as Katmai fell asleep, and I listened for the small sounds of baby breaths and snores, nearly inaudible over the din of snowshoes on ice. I checked on him obsessively, unsure of the fragility of this new life.

There are times when you realize that your life has irreversibly shifted. For me, those shifts have come walking—out in the wilderness, where the seemingly simple task of getting from point A to point B overtakes everything, wiping out all I once thought was important, filling the space of mountains and sky.

By the time Hig and I walked to the Aleutian Islands, none of that was new anymore. I thought I'd moved beyond the power of wilderness to change me. It already had. But that year of footsteps and storms brought the most profound shift of all, as we reenvisioned our lives over the course of four thousand miles.

Now I was suddenly a parent. Suddenly responsible for a brand-new life, in an everyday journey that upends the lives of hundreds of thousands of people every day. It was a shift that promised to be larger than anything we'd ever experienced. Except it wasn't really a shift at all. Without even knowing it, I'd been training for parenthood for years. Our journeys had taught me more than just wilderness skills. They had taught me to be good at transitions. To be adaptable. To embrace the immediate circumstances, and continue the journey under whatever those new conditions might be. That the inefficient choices and inevitable mistakes along the way will become the fondest memories.

The white snow that enveloped our yurt shrunk back to muddy brown, and then burst into a green filled with the whine of mosquitoes, the prick of salmonberry thorns, and the sharp smell of elderberry. Katmai stretched out from his days of curled slumber into a smiling, squealing baby, with a puzzled expression, fists full of grass, and a mouth full of gravel.

As the summer months slipped by, our new rhythm evolved. Hig or I would wrap our torso with a several-yard-long length of fabric, carefully knotting it into a shape that could hold a tiny human. From there, the steps proceeded in a never-ending cycle that grew more familiar with every outing.

Tuck baby into wrap, face into Mommy or Daddy's chest. Walk a few minutes until baby falls asleep. Continue until the baby wakes and screams.

Pluck him out, nurse him, and pop him back into the wrap, face out this time. Protect baby's eyes from the bushes as he gets a close-up tour of prickly spruce branches. Try to keep mosquitoes off the baby's face. Continue until baby screams.

Pluck him out, nurse him, and set him somewhere to chew on a stick. Then pop him back into the wrap, face in.

Repeat.

It seemed like a rhythm that could continue forever. We tested it, stretched it, each day hike a little longer, a little more difficult than the last, dragging our stream of summer visitors out into the woods along with us.

❧

Then we leaped farther—twenty miles east and two bays over, to the remote alpine reaches of Kachemak Bay State Park. We walked on ice. We walked past newborn lakes. We skated down slopes of scree, past cliffs scratched by vanished ice and decorated with mountain goats. We did all of this in the span of about four days, with our six-month-old son and my fifty-something-year-old mother.

"What do you mean there's probably a way?" she asked, as we puzzled over the map on an incline of gritty snow.

"I mean there's good chance this icefield has retreated a bit," I said, pointing at a white smudge on the topo map. "And that slope looks fairly steep, but also fairly smooth, so there might be a talus field on it somewhere that will get us down. And from there. . . ."

Narrow goat trails threaded us between cliffs and ice. Katmai watched and slept and giggled from his perch on our chests. And screamed. And fussed. And tried to wriggle out of the tiny rafts we were paddling. And tried to eat small rocks. And refused to go to sleep in the tent at night.

I winced at each yell, imagining the sound ringing through the thin walls of my mom's next-door tent. Hig walked back and forth and back and forth again, his feet crunching a well-worn path across a moonlit snowfield, with a crying baby snuggled against his chest.

Each time I tucked Katmai into the wrap, I looked back beyond my own memories into the pages of photo albums. My mom, with a long dark braid, hiking through the deserts of Utah, and me, a baby with white-blond hair, smiling from the frame of a Snugli carrier on her back. Her, my age now. Me, Katmai's age now.

When I was older, each summer brought pilgrimages to Washington's Cascade Mountains. While my brother and I carried barely more than our sleeping bags, I remember my mom propping her overloaded pack against a tree, sitting down to strap herself in, and then staggering up with a tremendous heave of leg muscles. We played rhyming games, and games of Twenty Questions that easily stretched into two hundred. She coaxed my little brother down the trail with M&M's.

I remembered making dolls out of lichen and twigs. Catching orange-bellied newts. Pulling my mother into the frigid water of an alpine lake so I could "paddle" a driftwood log across it. My father and I fishing with a scavenged bit of line and a piece of salami—then cleaning the six-inch trout out of sight of my squeamish mom. Huddling with my cousin in a leaking tent in an all-night rain. It was only a few weekends each summer, but those weekends are all that I remember.

As a kid, I'd never thought much about the work it took for my mom to drag us out there—the decades of commitment that stretched from packing babies and diapers into those babies' grown-up adventures. And now it was my turn.

⟋⟍

"I may not be fast, but I always get there," my mom commented, catching up to us on the crest of a steep ridge.

Hig peered over the edge at the fog-swirled valley below, trying to puzzle out some piece of a future route. I untwisted the wrap holding Katmai, who had started to cry.

"You're not slow. I'm the slow one, because I have to stop now and nurse him again," I pointed out. "I always say it doesn't matter how fast we walk, and now it *really* doesn't matter. You know—you did this all before."

"I never did *anything* like you guys do," she countered. "We always had trails."

"Sure. But remember those packs you used to carry? And you often took two kids by yourself."

At six months old, Katmai weighed seventeen pounds. His diapers and clothes were another four pounds. The extra food I needed to make milk for him added another few pounds on top of that. All told, one little baby was responsible for about twenty-five pounds of the eighty-five or so Hig and I were carrying between the two of us.

Katmai's need for nursing breaks, play breaks, and diaper changes was not at all timed with terrain, weather, or anything else. Anything within reach—rocks, grass, poisonous mushrooms—could go into his mouth. His patience with the unpleasant was three seconds long, ending in a wail of wordless and inscrutable complaint. Hot? Cold? Sleepy? Hungry? Bored?

With a baby strapped to my chest, I was perfectly positioned to spend my day nuzzling that sweet-smelling downy blond head. Perfectly positioned to spend my day tripping over my own invisible feet. I took every step twice as carefully—sometimes half as fast. With every patch of brush, I kept my arms extended to keep the branches from scratching Katmai's face.

But after pregnancy, I hadn't seen my feet in months anyway, so I shouldn't much miss them. Backpacking has always been an exercise in embracing inconvenience. We start out limited to the food and shelter we can carry on our backs, and then carry it through places usually steep, brushy, slippery, confusing, cold, and inhabited by bears—all the while forgoing the option to go inside, turn on a light, or run past the store. The inconvenience of parenthood should fit right in.

I stared across the crevassed expanse of ice—that white smudge on the topo map brought into reality. Hig and I passed our camera back and forth, eagerly snapping pictures of blue-white columns in misty clouds, and the abstract patterns formed by a fractured maze of crevasses. My mom pulled out her own camera—a near twin of ours—and we discussed lighting and camera settings briefly between the clicks of shutters. I tucked a bandanna over Katmai's head where he lay sleeping on my chest, protecting new baby skin from the glare of sun on ice. According to the topographic map, we were well beneath that ice.

Ice awes me. Growing up, I had always thought of glaciers as accents—shapely white markings that graced the tallest peaks of my Washington home. Until the moment in my first summer in Alaska, eight years earlier, when I climbed a ridge to look out over a corner of the Harding Icefield and saw that the mountains were nothing. They were tiny. They were measly triangles of rock in a vast sheet of crinkled white. The glacier was . . . more ice than I had ever imagined.

This was another corner of the Harding Icefield. Still as amazing as it had been eight years ago. And not all that large. On the scale of ice sheets, the Harding is a small one—getting smaller every year. On the maps we used to find our way, white blobs of glaciers crisscrossed our route at every turn. In reality, the glaciers spilling out over the edges of the icefield are shrunken or gone, turning navigation into a series of educated guesses.

Where our map marks "Southern Glacier," we know a rocky saddle we call "Southern Glacier Pass." The lakes we camped beside were gleaming-blue circles of newborn water, framed by newly exposed cliffs. Sharp rocks and mud piled on patches of dead ice. Tiny spots of green speckled the edge of rock fields, where lichens and grasses are expanding their range. In some places, we probably left the very first human footsteps. It's been sixty years since the maps were made. In another thirty years, Katmai might come here with his own child—and me as the adventurous grandma. What will we see?

⌒

This is how I first understood climate change. Not as skyrocketing graphs of burning oil, carbon dioxide concentrations, and global temperatures—though I knew those basics. But as the brand-new world on the shrinking edges of the ice. This is the world where climate change comes to life. Where it smacks you in the face with its incontrovertible reality.

Just a few miles away, as the water trickles down from the shrinking edge of the Harding Icefield, it flows past a stark gray landscape of dead spruce forests, killed by the bark beetle that thrives in warmer weather. Continuing downstream, that trickle adds a little bit of water to the sea, slowly rising to threaten coastal communities. Beyond that, I couldn't see the droughts and storms and ocean acidification, the fragile sea ice and crumbling permafrost, the struggling animals and the struggling people. But I know that they're there.

If Katmai comes back here as an adult, this alpine ridge might be an even more magical place to hike than it is today. But what will the rest of the world be like? Bringing a child into a world of rapid climate change might mean bringing him into a world of transformed politics, gleaming solar panels, and an economy where community has pushed aside consumption. Or a world of pain and extinction, upheaval and hardship. Or more likely, some of each scenario. The balance between them is our decision— one we're making every day, whether we think about it or not.

I couldn't help thinking about it. Having a baby personalized the future, ensuring I saw every one of those gloomy predictions through the screen of my own child's face.

~∽~

Hig skated down a scree slope, while Katmai grinned and giggled from his chest, utterly unconcerned by the clatter of rolling rocks. He had no complex worries about the future or the present. He trusted us. He trusted us to keep the bushes out of his face. He trusted us not to drop him on the boulders or ice. He trusted us to keep him warm and fed and dry. Katmai spent his days snuggling his parents and watching the world go by. Each place we stopped, he found new bushes to chew on and new rocks to investigate, his neurons weaving a pattern to mimic the universe.

"He's so patient!" I exclaimed, near the end of a long day of hiking.

"Actually, he's not patient at all," Hig pointed out. "He's just happy."

I wondered what impact it had on a baby to spend so much time looking at trees and rivers, rocks and berry bushes, tundra and rabbit tracks. Maybe he would grow to love the outdoors. Or maybe not. But he was too young to tell us, and too young to decide. Maybe wondering about the impact on Katmai was the wrong question altogether. He had joined a family of adventurers, therefore he comes on adventures, adapting to the circumstances of his birth like every baby in the world.

The journey had been less than a week, but as we settled back into ordinary life, we found that our dreams had grown. We had stopped thinking of babysitters, and stopped thinking of waiting. Maybe real expeditions were possible with children after all.

2: Life in the Yurt

"AREN'T YOUR FEET COLD?" Sarah asked, scooting closer to the woodstove.

The fire flicked orange light across the floor. Splintered wood balanced in a neat stack several feet away. Outside, the thud of Hig's splitting maul sprayed a halo of bark and wood chips over the snow. A winter's worth of splitting builds a crust so thick that the snow beneath it might last the summer.

"Not really," I shrugged. "I mean, I do wear socks inside." The air outside was probably fifteen degrees Fahrenheit, swirling into the space under the yurt with bicycles and drifts of snow, before seeping up through the protective wrapper of Tyvek, insulation, and sagging plywood that formed our floor. The air inside might have been sixty degrees, but the floor—through the holes in my worn-out hiking socks—was colder. I barely felt it. The real purpose of the socks was to protect my feet from squashed bits of muffin, sharp toys, and forgotten puddles of melting snow. But Sarah couldn't know that. I'd swept before she got here. Katmai, ten months old now, gripped a piece of red and yellow plywood with bare toes, concentrating on his newfound balance, not seeming to notice the cold.

The woodstove in the center of the yurt is our source of warmth.

Sarah was visiting us courtesy of the *New York Times*, from New York City, the other side of the world. She'd flown over three thousand miles in a series of smaller and smaller planes, before rumbling onto Seldovia's gravel airstrip in the narrow sliver of light offered by a dark and cold December. Three miles on a winding road, a few hundred yards on a packed-snow footpath, and she was at our yurt.

I thought I was used to interviews. We hadn't journeyed quietly—blogging and writing and filming and giving slideshows in school auditoriums and chatting with reporters on snowy streets and in the warm comfort of radio studios. I could anticipate all the usual questions about cold, bears, food, and how could anyone tolerate an entire year barely more than an arm's length from her spouse? But Sarah was different. She wasn't here because of our expeditions. Her piece was for the "Home" section of the newspaper. I'd never read it, but I imagined the articles therein covering something much closer to carefully placed doilies and fancy chandeliers than dump-scavenged furniture and a floor cluttered with grimy baby toys.

But Sarah hadn't come for the decor. She was here for the outhouse. She was here because what we saw as ordinary life was something her readers would see as anything but.

༄

Our town, Seldovia, isn't an island, but visitors often mistake it for one. The road ends at Homer, 120 miles south of Anchorage in Southcentral Alaska. From there, we're fifteen miles away as the Cessna flies or the ferry runs. Only three or four hundred people live in town, depending on exactly whom you count and when you count them. There are twenty-seven thousand New Yorkers for every Seldovian.

We are not remote. By Alaska standards, we're a solid medium-sized village with just a touch of the middle-of-nowhere flavor that characterizes much of the state. Seldovia has around twenty-five miles of road, running from the dump to an abandoned chrome mine, and a fleet of rusted old trucks and four-wheelers to drive it. It's the kind of place where everyone leaves the keys in the ignition—there's nowhere a stolen car could go.

At the dump, workers watch what shows up with a calculated thrift, flagging down or calling up likely recipients with news of a discarded window, a culvert, a cupboard and dresser, a pair of kids' boots. At the post office, the postmistress lets Katmai sit on the counter, punching buttons to produce both official and ridiculous receipts. As soon as I reach my chair in the town's only restaurant, the waitress brings me an Americano coffee and Katmai a small dish of blueberries. Here it's expected you'll wave to every car on the road, certain that you'll recognize many of them. My husband grew up here. We moved next door to his mother, Dede, sharing a piece of land. When I first got here, I felt like I'd taken my fancy twenty-first-century education and moved straight back into the nineteenth.

Seldovia is full of carpenters, fishermen, hunters, kayakers, gardeners, skiers, and in the summer, tourists. The residents hail from a scattering of mostly northern states: Minnesota, Michigan, Montana, Maine. . . . Some are Native Alaskan. Some were raised here. But others have roots here not much longer than my own.

Alaska is a state of transplants. More than 70 percent of the adults who live here now were born somewhere else. Some come to work in the oil fields. Some come for wilderness, or fishing, or a summer of adventure. Most disappear as quickly as they came, driven back by homesickness, jobs, skimpy dating prospects, dark winters, or the collision of romantic dreams with the unpicturesque reality of tattered tarps, rusting oil drums, and derelict cars. A few of them stay, joining the Native people, who've been here for a few thousand years, and the children of gold rushers and pioneers who've been Alaskans for a few decades. America's wildest frontier has always held a special place in the dreams of misfits and adventurous spirits—pulling us to the end of the road and beyond—into a way of life that's hard to come back from. I stay, as many do, because I'd rather be Alaskan than anything else.

Careers are fluid here. Being a former molecular biologist turned adventurer/writer/consultant doesn't raise any eyebrows. "How do you make money?" is a separate question from "What do you do?" Subsistence is a mark of pride rather than of poverty. Social classes collapse into a mishmash of XtraTuf rubber boots and grubby raincoats, where fishermen become college professors and oil workers swap roles with homesteading hippies. Where they *are* the homesteading hippies.

Alaska is a self-important club, where provincialism runs rampant and longtime residents hold up their years as a point of pride. The rest of the country can be abbreviated to "Outside," with a capital O, sometimes with a disparaging tone and sometimes matter-of-factly, as if it were printed on the map that way. Maybe we are a club. There are so few of us. Hundreds of miles from Seldovia, meeting a new Alaskan, I'll find we have at least one acquaintance in common. Where everyone knows us, there is no need for constant explanation. Where misfits gather, it's easy to feel more normal. More than anywhere else I've lived, in Alaska I feel like I belong.

We're a club drawn together by both our distance and our difference, where film crews flock to our bears and wolves, our fishermen and pilots— our picturesque bizarreness. Sarah's visit seemed in a similar vein.

⌁

"Why did you choose to live in a yurt?" she asked me.

With its starburst of rafters, lattice-crossed windows, and circular form, the yurt proclaims its difference as soon as you step inside, as if the structure itself is making some kind of statement about our life. But for Hig and me, the yurt was more expedient than interesting. At the beginning, it was nothing more than walls and warmth, in quick and affordable versions.

We'd begun the process a year and a half before Sarah's visit, struggling to construct a platform that was round, level, and unlikely to collapse.

"Is that close enough?" Hig asked, from the other end of the long beam.

"I think this side's too high again," I yelled back.

Five months pregnant at the time, I stood in a dusty pit of mud and gravel at the edge of the driveway, peering at the level on the top of a thick spruce beam, wondering how everything had managed to become off kilter. For someone who never had trouble with calculus, seemingly straight-forward measurements of inches and feet always seemed to go wrong. I yearned for the simplicity of our tent, where any mistakes could be fixed by a simple tug on a string, one knot untied and redone.

We had moved onto a piece of my mother-in-law Dede's three acres, buying in with her on the property and hacking out a twenty-four-foot circle in the salmonberries and devil's club. Three miles out the road from downtown Seldovia, we are below a mountain and above a clearcut, with a view of Cook Inlet and the volcanoes beyond. Our loop of unlabeled road forms a small neighborhood shared with nine other houses, each on a similar piece of land.

The beam I leveled would hold up a seven-foot-tall platform, which would in turn hold up a yurt. We had built it two months before the snow would begin to fall. Six months before our first child would be born. We had to live somewhere. The yurt had arrived as a lumpy bundle of cloth and sticks, on a chilly November day, in the back of a pickup truck that had come on the ferry. I cleared the snow off our platform, as the lattice unfolded around it like a giant baby gate. The yurt went up in half a day.

We began in a yurt because it was easy. We stayed in the yurt because we grew to love it.

Sarah was sleeping in our tiny guest shed, a minute's walk up the unplowed driveway, transformed to a snowshoe path in the winter. Before she came down the next morning, I swept again. I called the dog, Panda, inside to finish the crumbs of toast from Katmai's breakfast, then wiped up the line of wet prints left by her snowy feet. I heated a kettle of water for another pot of coffee, and pulled back the curtain that serves as our bedroom wall to wake up Hig. I set our little rocking chair by the woodstove for our guest, as the fire's heat pushed back against the circle of chill that had crept in overnight.

Life in the yurt is life in a single, crowded room. When I work, I sit with my laptop on a table that doubles as a surface for family dinners, starting seedlings, squishing playdough, and sewing gear. Our sink drains into a pipe that empties into the bushes. The faucet does nothing. Wind rattles the flexible walls. Rain drums loudly on our fabric roof, replaced in this season by the shuddering crashes of sliding snow. We heat the space with already dead trees, first chainsawed by Hig, then dragged across the snow in a heavy black sled, crushing the prints left by his snowshoes. Finally, they are split, stacked, and fed into the woodstove at the center of the yurt. A hundred yards up the driveway, Dede lives in a small cabin not much bigger, and similarly lacking amenities. A tiny heated shed just large enough for a bed serves as the guest quarters on the compound. Panda, Dede's enthusiastic black lab/collie mix, runs freely between the buildings. Our outhouse is a stone's throw away, across the trail. A stone's throw in the other direction, our water comes from a ten-foot-deep well.

Chips flew from the ice axe as I widened the hole that had refrozen overnight, lowering a glass jar on a string and dipping water into a bucket, while Katmai watched from the wrap on my back. Brute labor for a simple glass of water. Was that what Sarah was looking for? It painted a pioneering picture that I tried to shrug off, explaining that a well casing, a lid, and a pump lay somewhere in our future—somewhere in a long list of tinkering improvements that haunts any homeowner's dreams.

At our yurt, the lights come on with the flip of a switch. The trail that forms our front yard is also a utilities right-of-way, where powerlines run up the hill to a communications tower nine hundred feet above us. The internet comes on with similar ease, a receiving dish high on a spruce tree enabling everything from research to web meetings to streaming movies. We live in that 450-square-foot room, and we work in it too, doing writing, consulting work, and science, in a bizarre combination of rustic and modern life.

The sound of crunching snow heralded Dede's arrival on our porch, peering through the window on our door.

"Come in!"

She opened the door a crack. "I've already got my snowshoes on," she explained. "I'm just heading to town for a few hours. Do you need anything?"

"Not today, I don't think. I was thinking of making salmon and berry crisp for dinner tonight, maybe around 6:30."

"Should I bring something?"

"No, I've got it. See you in a bit."

Dede's arrival in Seldovia, decades ago, was a real adventure. She moved here in the 1970s, with Hig's father, Craig, when Hig was just a baby. They knew just one pair of friends in town. Craig had visited once. Dede had never even set foot here before they began the long drive from Washington. They had almost no money, and no family for thousands of miles. They didn't stay together, but they both stayed in Seldovia. Dede has held jobs ranging from cannery work to T-shirt printing to alcoholism prevention to her current job as a special-ed aide in the school. She's lived in an apartment, and in a house she and Craig built themselves, accessible only by boat or foot trail. When they split up in Hig's childhood, Craig stayed in that house, while Dede moved through a new series of ancient houses and modern cabins, each with its own particular quirks. Finally she built her own place in Seldovia on the land we share. She's lived without running water for much of her adult life. She does dishes efficiently without it.

Dede's presence here smoothed our own arrival—making it almost embarrassingly easy when set against the standard stories of living in a wall tent while clearing and building on your own land from scratch. Those are the stories of many of our friends. Instead, we share the inconveniences of this particular chunk of land with Dede—its long unplowed driveway, west winds, and drifts of snow—and we share nearly everything else. The chest freezer under our yurt. Her garden tools and buckets. The well. Panda, who considers all of us part of her pack. The view. Dede will do errands for us on her more frequent trips to town. She'll watch Katmai for an hour or two when she gets home from work. In return, most nights I cook dinner for all of us—pulling the table into the middle of the yurt so we can all eat around it, as one big family.

☙

Our home is tiny yet enormous. When the *New York Times* photographer visited, about a week before Sarah arrived, we loaned him a pair of snowshoes. The still-fresh tracks of our neighbors (two people and one large-pawed dog) led us across the ice of a tucked-away lake, then into the gully of Wadsworth Creek, which slices a short wild path from the mountains to the ocean, only one road to note its passing. Katmai rode in a rainbow-colored wrap on my back, happily watching Panda bury her nose in the drifts of powder, snuffling for the hidden holes of voles and shrews.

We posed for photographs. We tromped back to the yurt along the packed-down furrow we'd just made, stripped off the snowshoes, kicked the snow off our boots, and settled down to chat around the crackling wood-stove. If I'd cleared the toys off the floor, it could have been a scene from a weekend ski lodge visit. When the article was eventually published, the photos did remind me of a ski lodge. The text was different, more "purpose-ful self-deprivation" or "uncomfortable idealists" than "happy people who manage to live as if they are always on a ski vacation." I felt just a little embarrassed to read it, wishing there had been a bit more snowshoeing in the story, and maybe a little less of the cold floor. I wasn't embarrassed that I live with an outhouse, but I worried that readers might think that the outhouse was the whole point.

I'm not a luddite. Just a cheapskate.

My lack of a shower and a toilet seemed to me to be a calculated and perfectly sensible trade-off between convenience and freedom. Freedom to stay home with a kid or to take off adventuring with him for months at a time. Freedom to work a lot or not work much at all. Freedom to work for free or work on my own schedule on the work I feel is important at the moment.

We live on the doorstep of wilderness, with a million-dollar view, space for a garden, a close-knit community, a cheap and debt-free lifestyle, and a schedule nearly entirely of our own making. Could I have all that *and* all the conveniences and comforts of urban life? Maybe, with enough money. But what would I give up to earn it?

Sarah's published article prompted a response on the online site Gawker, which proclaimed that our lifestyle made us "the most annoying *New York Times* couple ever." The online commenters busied themselves trying to expose us as wealthy fakers with a huge house just beyond the view of the camera. Almost universally, what they imagined was their own world, hiding just out of sight. We must be playing at "living rough" for a few years, planning one day to flee back to "civilization." We must really be hiding a furnace, a trust fund, a car. Hiding city life beneath a veneer of snow.

Seldovia folks just thought the article was amusing. The truth was best stated by an Alaskan reporter, in an article published a couple of years later. We are, in fact, "almost boringly normal." We could have led these readers to dozens of other families who lived with wood heat and outhouses. People who'd raised children in smaller spaces than ours, in cabins built with their own hands from trees they cut and milled themselves. People off the electric grid and more than our short walk from the town's plowed roads. People who lived a far more homesteading, hardscrabble existence than we did. People who did everything that we did, only more beautifully, with a much longer track record behind them.

Giving away most of our possessions and walking for a year before setting up our "real life" put Hig and me in the unusual position of building a life from the ground up. Each choice was one we had to make from scratch—from where we got our power to where we got our food and whether we should hire a backhoe to dig out our well. We were faced with our own ideals, finances, and time at every turn. We wanted to build a life that was meaningful and happy, and that left a light footprint on the earth. How much of that we achieved was entirely up to us.

3: Learning to Fish

FISHING POLES BRISTLED from the panniers of a friend's bike. Just behind her, another friend pulled two babies in a bright yellow trailer. Katmai (nearly one and a half now) rode on my back as I pedaled. Finally, one more friend clattered over the cobbles with buckets and bags. We were a parade in scuffed rubber boots—four women and three babies bouncing over the washed-out logging roads standing between us and a lagoon full of salmon.

"More ride! More ride!" Katmai yelled from over my shoulder as I briefly dismounted, negotiating the bike through a steep ditch. A few years ago, I'd walked this route when it was a foot trail through the forest. Now the trail signs led to piles of logging slash, a lonely strip of trees wrapping a small creek, and spruce seedlings reaching through a tangle of berries. The curves followed by the logging trucks sliced their efficiency through the former woods, shrinking the space to a fraction of my memories.

We parked the bikes, switching the babies to carriers and backpacks. The last ridge, lying beyond Native corporation lands on a state park, was passable only by a narrow path through deep spruce forest. Head-high devil's club bristled along its edges, and we clambered over and under the logs that had fallen over the trail.

Her daughter on her back, Kari leans over to pull up a giant halibut.

It was time to introduce the little ones to one of the rituals of an Alaskan summer—getting your salmon. More to the point, it was time to introduce myself to the ritual. Even before I lived in Seldovia, I'd spent enough summers in Alaska to get my hands into a few slimy fish carcasses. I'd cleaned salmon, canned salmon, frozen salmon, smoked salmon, cooked salmon, and eaten salmon, but I'd never caught my own.

◦∕◦

At Tutka Lagoon, angular gray rocks decorated with barnacles and popweed sloped gently down to the water. The tide was low, and the lagoon was smooth and empty. I hefted my borrowed rod. After a quick lesson from my friend Damara, I started casting with gusto, snagging various pieces of seaweed and rocks from my perch on the gravel beach. At that point, I could have easily blamed my failure on positioning. We couldn't see the fish from shore. Even the experienced fisherwomen couldn't cast far enough to reach their hooks beyond the shallows to where the fish swam thickly.

The tide rose, lifting kelp and eelgrass to flutter in the currents, pouring a stream of boats through the narrow channel that connected the lagoon to the larger bay beyond. Soon the calm pocket of water buzzed with the sound of a dozen skiffs, looping in pursuit of the schools of red salmon.

Everyone loves red (sockeye) salmon—prized occupants of smokehouses and plates—lake-beach spawners that can run in the millions. But we weren't at a lake. Our corner of the Kenai Peninsula is cut off from the flatlands by crumpled mountains, deep fjords, and sheets of ice, where nearly every lake is a tiny alpine jewel far beyond the reach of fish. The reds at Tutka are an artificial production. Around thirty thousand fish return here each year, with nowhere to go but this dead-end lagoon. They clump together in mutual confusion, abandoned by their homing instincts to the wavering shadows of fishermen. Some are caught for their eggs and sperm—parents to the next generation. Others are caught for "cost recovery," sold to processors to help pay for the hatchery. The rest are left to a crowd of locals sporting rubber boots and snagging rods—only Alaskans allowed.

Sun gleamed on the blue-green water and the fishing lines snaking out from every boat. It flashed on slippery silver scales and on blood-smeared decks. Did all of those boaters see the longing in our repetitive fruitless casts? Thirty minutes in, and their limit already reached, a couple from Homer invited Damara and me on board to try our luck from the water. Katmai snacked on crackers as he stared at the salmon in the bottom of the boat, their eyes glazed over, their tails twitching spasmodically in a puddle of blood. I stood on the bench next to him, eyes on the water, as I carefully listened to a series of instructions on the right rhythm of reeling and jerking. I listened again as they tried to explain how I was still doing it wrong.

Snagging is a fishing style that most closely resembles harpooning with a fishing rod. A heavy triple-barbed hook is hurled past a visible school of fish, then yanked back through them in the hope of snagging flesh. Instead of hoping a fish will bite a lure, snaggers hope their lure will bite the fish, transforming the thrill of the chase to the thrill of filling the freezer as quickly as possible. On the other end of the boat, Damara wore her own baby on her back, the awkwardness of that arrangement doing nothing to slow down her efficient casts and the quick rhythm of fish being pulled on board.

Each person who shows up at Tutka Lagoon is allowed to snag six fish a day. Some people fish bleary-eyed across Alaska's long summer evenings, staying through midnight to double their quota of fish. Even the babies qualified for a share. We stood in the crowd of gas-powered motor boats, bristling with pale-faced people holding modern fishing rods, targeting salmon concentrated here only by the presence of a hatchery. Is this what modern subsistence looks like? It bore little resemblance to the ancient traditions of handmade nets and scattered fish camps. But already, I felt like I *needed* these salmon. I could buy food from the grocery store whenever I wanted, all year-round. But a winter without salmon? The fish we put away in the summer were a key component of February dinners. The same was true for most of our friends and neighbors. And I really wanted to catch one!

Tutka is easy but not idiot-proof. Long after everyone else in the boat had gotten their fish, I continued my fruitless casts, sending the line out in a zipping rush over and over again, merely hoping to intersect a fish. Modern technology still wasn't making up for my lack of skill.

"Here, try my sunglasses," Damara offered, done fishing. "They're polarized, so you can see the fish a little better."

Finally, I glimpsed the waving shapes of gray beneath the green. I cast just beyond the thick school of salmon, reeling back through them with a series of staccato jerks, pulling enthusiastically with more muscle than I could possibly need, imagining something more solid than ocean at the end of my hook. Still nothing. I hadn't managed to borrow Damara's skills with the sunglasses. But after a few more minutes, it suddenly worked. Dangling in the air, the fish startled me with its impossibly slippery thrashing. I had one small, beautiful red salmon. A few minutes later, I pulled in a larger one.

"I think it's about time to go," Damara pointed out, her baby fussing while Katmai squirmed on the seat. My appetite for the hunt was barely whetted, but I nodded in agreement like a sensible mom.

"Eeeet fisssh! Eeeet fisssh!" I tried to head off Katmai as he ran toward the row of glistening salmon on the beach, stiffening in the heat as we hurried to get them home. We pulled out plastic bags of melting ice, cramming salmon into cloth shopping bags, bike panniers, now-empty lunch bags, and the diaper compartments of baby backpacks, the fish tails protruding from their half-zipped pockets. On the trail, I realized that my poor fishing skills were not altogether a bad thing. Salmon are heavy.

Back at the truck, Damara added a few of her fish to my bucket, shrugging off my half-hearted protest with an assertion that she could get more. One of my other friends threw in a few of her own, noting that since she and her husband fished commercially, she could get as many fish as she wanted. They all could. On another day, I saw Damara carry two toddlers (both heavier than mine) the entire length of the Tutka Bay trail, one on each hip, and catch fish from shore when she got there. My friends' generosity was coupled with a confidence I didn't have—that fish were valuable, but easy. They could afford not to care about these few.

⁓

Sawhorses and a board formed a makeshift filleting table in my driveway, where I filled ziplock bags with gleaming red flesh and wondered if the drippings would bring the bears. The bags dropped with a wet slap into the empty chest freezer. Should I go back? In the swarm of skiffs and fishing rods, I was caught up in the excitement of the hunt—imagining the taste of that rich pink flesh.

All I wanted to do was to catch as many fish as I could. But afterward, I had mixed feelings about getting our fish from Tutka Lagoon. About eating hatchery fish at all. In Washington, where I grew up, hatcheries had been largely a disaster. Built with the intention of helping out the salmon stocks that had been depleted by dams, fishing, and development, the hatcheries in Washington had been easy promises to make—easier than making the world a friendlier place for wild fish. Expensive promises, though. Ineffective promises. Promises that often further depleted the very wild fish the hatcheries had been intended to save.

But maybe not all hatcheries are the same. The Tutka hatchery was planted in a dead-end lagoon far away from the streams and lakes that host wild red salmon. Maybe here the fry won't outcompete wild ones for food. Yet it seemed impossible to dump such a large number of anything into such a small piece of water and expect it not to change the ecosystem. I hope the impact will be smaller. But I'm not sure what the costs of this salmon "enhancement" are—to fish or to people. Who, if anyone, is paying to fill my freezer?

In some parts of Alaska, like Bristol Bay, the entire salmon stock is wild, but here in Cook Inlet there are more people and fewer fish. The inlet is thick with small pink salmon, strewing their spawned-out bodies along every coastal creek. But people prefer the larger, tastier, and higher-priced reds. Cook Inlet's hatcheries drive up their numbers. The harvest of the more-prized fish is nearly half composed of these "enhanced" stocks.

❧

We filled the freezer enough. A few more fish from Tutka, and a few bucketsful bought from a setnet fisherman in Seldovia Bay, catching fish bound for hatcheries and wild lakes alike. Subsistence is real here. Not as a total separation from the modern world of shipped-in food and manufactured goods, but as one little piece of independence. One small piece where we depend instead on the world right in front of us.

Our power comes from a line strung all the way across the bay, beginning at a distant natural gas plant and at a dam in the mountains. Our heat comes from firewood—dead spruce snags on the slopes surrounding us. Our pantry is stocked with rice and coffee and olive oil, but the freezer is filled with salmon, blueberries, and nettles. Living here, we learn the ripening time of each local blueberry patch and the tricks to find the driest wood. The more we depend on the land around us, the closer I feel tied to it.

Even the language reflects that dependence. It's not just "going fishing," it's "putting up fish" or "getting your fish," as if the salmon in the sea belong to us before we even catch them—interdependence giving way to a sense of ownership. It's easy to get caught up in the cycle of subsistence. Getting food for free is addictive—intoxicating. Sometimes it makes sense. Sometimes, when I find myself stuck in a berry thicket, fingers stained purple, bucket overflowing but unwilling to leave because I see *just a few more berries over there!*—it seems more like a compulsion. The culture in Seldovia is more intensely local than anywhere else I've lived. People eat fish snagged with their own hooks, and vegetables dug with their own muddy fingers. They drink water from their own wells, and build with wood from trees they cut themselves, in a cycle of mock-primitiveness that could seem smug and virtuous if anyone thought about it that way. But they don't. It just seems normal, sensible, and frugal.

This faux-subsistence is no deeper than the thickness of a salmon fillet. We are not an island. Every grain of rice in the pantry, every car tire and plastic bag, and nearly every single purchased item in the entire state is made "Outside." Alaska is a place that deals in raw resources. We export oil, fish, metal, wood, pretty pictures, and the idea of a frontier. We eat our moose and fish and berries. And that's where our economy, and our self-sufficiency, ends.

~⁄~

A few months after the salmon-catching adventure, I clutched the loops on Katmai's life vest, as the small skiff rocked back and forth in the water. My friend Kari, her own one-year-old strapped to her back, hung over the side of the boat, pulling the line as another friend, Chris, held the gaff. Hig was at the bow—not quite as useless as I was but close. All were balanced with a nervous tension, as a speckled brown slab slowly emerged with each arm's length of rope. We watched our boat shrink with each pull, the halibut growing.

Halibut are big business in Alaska. Commercial fishermen get high prices for their prized flesh. A fleet of charter boats from Homer carries fishing tourists from across the country, dreaming of halibut that outweigh themselves.

We were dreaming of dinner. This was a subsistence long line, another locals-only fishery that redirected the enterprise from sport to food. On a long line, a series of hooks rests far down in the water column, each with a chunk of octopus or herring for bait. We were pulling the line Kari had set, pulling up empty hooks one by one, hoping to add a few bags of halibut to the red salmon filling our freezers. The boat gave a sudden lurch, sending Chris stumbling backward as the weight of the fish balanced on the rail, then flopped into the bow. Katmai in my arms, I lunged toward the other side, trying to balance the weight of the tilting skiff before it tipped all of us into the bay.

She filled the boat, her brown skin glistening, her mouth gaping, her 120 pounds of muscle shuddering the boards with a flap of her tail. We clung to the skiff's edges, moving gingerly, knowing that one fish was stronger than any of us humans. Chris skirted her powerful tail, moved in with a long knife, and sliced through the halibut's throat, pouring blood to mix with the slime, ropes, and seawater at the bottom of the skiff.

Katmai watched from his perch by the steering wheel: "Dat big fisssh!"

"Yes," I agreed. "That's a very, very big fish."

"Thank you, mama," Kari concluded, looking at the gasping halibut.

We'd almost decided to throw her back, but the hook was lodged deep. We weren't sure she'd survive the release. That much fish would feed our families for months, and a few friends besides.

Back at the dock, I perched Katmai on the cleaning table, where he watched Kari and Chris at work, their slender fillet knives carving huge slabs of white-pink meat. Kari and her family are summer Seldovians and winter Girdwoodites, migrating around 150 miles twice a year. She plays fiddle in summer concerts and at fall parties and lives in a hand-built cabin a ways out the road. Chris lives a few miles from us in another hand-built cabin, bakes round loaves of crusty bread for potlucks, and can keep his compost going nearly all winter long. And in addition to building houses and catching halibut, they both know how to fillet fish. The fact that I forgot my knife prevented me from betraying my own ignorance. I took pictures and stuffed chunks of fish into ziplock bags.

We offered fish back and forth to each other—"Here, you take this one." "No, you can take it." We crammed bags of translucent flesh into overfull coolers that were the picture of abundance. But that picture was an illusion. Throughout Alaska waters, juvenile halibut are teeming, but the larger fish—the spawners, the ones that commercial and sports fishermen prize, the ones like ours—are mysteriously scarce. The ocean is opaque, mysterious, and difficult to monitor. Past estimates turned out to be wrong. The total biomass of halibut—the weight of all those fish in the ocean—is nothing like what the fisheries models say it should be. Baby halibut are disappearing before they can grow. Are they pulled up as bycatch in the trawl fishery and tossed back dead overboard? Is their food declining? Are they losing out in competition to other fish, like pollock or arrowtooth flounder? Are we simply catching too many of them?

The answer to all of these questions is probably "yes," at least in part. So charter boat operators blame commercial halibut fishermen who blame bycatch from the pollock trawl fishery. Quotas are ratcheting down, setting off a bitter fight between the parties who make their living from the fish.

We try to learn from the mistakes of the past. Alaska has vanished herring stocks, bays fished out of crab, and struggling king salmon runs. But it also has teeming salmon runs, bays that turn white with herring eggs, and still-abundant fisheries all over the state. It has computer models, state biologists, and regulations.

The key words are "sustainable yield." Biologists struggle to tease out the shifting mysteries of each year's fish stock, guessing just how many we can catch without reducing their numbers, attacked from all quarters whenever their answers are inconvenient. Regulators may bend to political pressure. Warming and acidifying oceans constantly change the parameters of every model. The more effective technology of monitoring and science goes head to head with the more effective technology of killing fish.

Our forays into subsistence put us right up close with all its uncomfortable issues. But all the food we didn't catch—those bags of rice and bottles of oil—came from thousands of miles away, from places where the wild ecosystem has long since been pushed out by people. Where fertilizer runs into streams, groundwater is depleted, soil erodes, and ten calories of fossil fuel produce one calorie of food. It's harder to ignore the impacts close to home. Using a wild place is often what drives people to know it and love it. That connection brings all the political clout that conservation has in Alaska, where the wilderness still seems inexhaustible. Fishermen need the fish to come back next year. We still have room to get some things right.

৩∕৹

Back at the yurt, I piled bags of halibut on top of bags of salmon in the freezer, personally responsible for nothing beyond the freezing part. Many of the people I knew these days were part of a crowd that seemed to already know how to do everything useful, yet never acted superior. The Native residents of Seldovia began in a culture of subsistence. And many of the white residents have more than a little of the homesteader mentality to them. It seemed like nearly everyone we knew could build a cabin, catch fish, hunt game, grow food, gather plants, smoke salmon, cook excellent food from scratch, fell a tree, split wood, fix a car, maintain a boat, and wire a house.

My debt to the fish was a debt to the community as well. Everyone had so much to share, and so much to teach us. How could I really belong to the community if I had no way to contribute? Bring me halibut, and I can help you set up a website. Help with the yurt platform, and I can edit a grant proposal or give a presentation to the school kids. But it never seemed to shake out quite that neatly. I wanted to eat halibut far more often than my friends wrote grants. I may be a rural resident and wilderness junkie, but I'm constantly reminded that I am a newcomer to this life. Sometimes I wish I knew some way to give back that was more concrete—and closer to home.

4: Summer Roots

At the end of June, we found the sun sliding over the ocean in an endless
sunset, the salmonberry bushes bursting in pink blossoms, and the vegetable
seedlings planted a month earlier struggling beneath a vigorous blanket
of weeds. Officially, summer had barely started, but it seemed like it was
already slipping away from us. Summer in Alaska is chaotic, hurried, and
overstuffed. The long months of winter dormancy lead up to a short and
furious burst of growth and activity—for wildlife and humans alike. After
seven months of winter, our expectations were built so high that even the
infinite daylight never seemed like enough.

"Ow-site! Ow-site!" Katmai ran to the door, stretched up to his full
sixteen-month-old height, failing to reach the doorknob he didn't know
how to turn, holding a boot he didn't know how to put on. In late morning,
shafts of sunlight were just beginning to reach around the trees. "Outside"
was one of his only two-syllable words.

An enthusiastic and unbalanced sprint brought him down the short
path to the garden, where I joined him, kneeling to the perpetual chore of
pulling horsetails from between the tiny carrot seedlings. Katmai stared over
my shoulder. Before he could help me, I diverted his curiosity by tossing

Katmai waters the young cabbages.

horsetails in a plastic dump truck and listening to the clatter as he pulled it down the rough gravel driveway. Our yard is the driveway—a slice of gravel cut into a ridge—lined by patches of garden I constantly hack clear from the salmonberries, fireweed, grass, elderberry, alder, currants, and ferns that seek to engulf them. Beyond the garden's edge, that exuberance of growth blends into a deceptively soft-looking green. Five hundred feet below us, the ruffled water of Cook Inlet sweeps to the blue-distant volcanoes on its farther shore.

We live on three acres, and I dream of the day it might all be edible. Each spring, in the muck of meltout, I prowl our patches of wild blueberries with thick gloves and a pair of pruning shears, cutting off devil's club before they can sprout leaves. I transplant strawberries in patchy clumps along the long driveway, relocating their stringy red runners along the edge, encouraging them to take over from the barren slopes. There are raspberries too. I've stolen wild nettles from a nearby creek, planting them in a damp haven beneath spruce trees and alders. I've brought home edible beach plants to an unusual elevation, hoping they might thrive. And I've poured the rest of that enthusiasm into the garden.

I finished up the weeding, grabbed a few radishes that seemed big enough to eat, and began to coax Katmai the sixty yards that separated my garden from Dede's. My mud-smudged notebook sat open on a stump by the gardening gloves, dutifully noting planting and harvest dates, mishaps, and all my do-better-next-years.

May 9—Trays of seedlings hardened off on the porch while I shoveled snow off the garden beds, trying to hasten the arrival of spring.

May 19—I went out to the garden in the morning to find that some kind of bird has chomped every single broccoli and cabbage start. I left the remains limping along in the garden.

June 28—The perennial sorrel towers over all my annuals, adding a tang to every dinner. Broccoli rabe and the first few radishes join them.

I found Dede arranging rocks in the walls that terraced her garden. "Radish?" I held out the one Katmai hadn't bitten into. We shared the gardens like we shared the rest of the land, passing seed catalogs back and forth in the winter and seed packets back and forth in the spring, attempting to divine the best spot for every vegetable. Harvesting and eating were nearly always communal. Watering and weeding often were as well. While my garden was a well-documented series of off-kilter rectangles, Dede's had flowers, rock walls lining winding paths, decorative pottery—beauty among vegetables.

She pinched the taproot from the radish and brushed it off on her pants. "I have swallows in the house, on my porch, but not in the guest shed yet this year. I did see a pair checking it out this morning, though. Are there swallows down by you?"

I shrugged. I'd cheered on the swallows in their swooping darts for mosquitoes, but I hadn't yet noticed where or whether they'd set up to nest. I was always struck by Dede's noticing. I'd take the same hike a dozen times, then she'd come along once and point out a dozen things I'd never seen before. She knew it was the Steller's jays that had pulled up the broccoli when I was still suspecting the sparrows.

☙

A month later, I slowly waddled between the well and the garden, struggling under the weight of two five-gallon buckets. Katmai ducked under the old fishing net that keeps the dog from using the garden as a runway, filling his little blue watering can from one of my buckets, then proceeding to pour the lot on both of our boots. I cringed to see my effort evaporate, then slopped out a little more myself as I poured from the bucket into a larger watering can. I ignored the weeds springing up beneath the kale as I gave both a good dousing. At least my vegetables were taller than the weeds.

Half of the garden beds were two years old. The rest were newer. My success was about what you'd expect from a brand-new gardener with a three- or four-month growing season. I was motivated but still shy. At potlucks, I nosed around neighbors' yards, measuring their plants against my own, not quite willing to corner anyone and ask how they did it. I trolled for pieces of secondhand wisdom, sidling closer to the many garden-related conversations I overheard. A homesteader-fisherman who'd been doing all of this since Hig was a baby talked about how he buried salmon beneath next year's vegetables: "At least a foot deep, and then the bears won't bother them. I've been doing it for years." I saw other neighbors warming their plants beneath gauzy tents of row-cover cloth or gathering washed-up kelp to strew on in the fall.

My raised garden beds were lined with discarded scraps of scraggly two-by-sixes, and filled with somewhat scraggly plants. The cabbages and kohlrabi and broccoli were scattered in an unintentional randomness, labels lost in transplanting. I never knew their seedlings all looked the same. I'd only eaten kohlrabi once in my life, from Dede's garden the year before. It was delicious. It was something that would grow here. I wasn't too shy to ask her for tips, learning the list of Alaska-friendly crops. She was happy to share: "All the brassicas do well here, and carrots and peas and lettuces, and you can get green beans to grow in a cold frame. I've done tomatoes on the porch, but they really need a greenhouse. In the catalog, it's good to look for varieties that will mature in sixty or seventy days, because the season length is the real problem here."

It was the seed catalogs that pushed me over the edge. Sending photos of green lettuce, orange carrots, and red beets—in all their dazzling varieties—to someone sitting in four feet of snow eating wilted and expensive broccoli is like advertising hot pizza to wet backpackers a hundred miles from town. I like to think I'm not swayed by advertising. But I clearly had twice as many seeds as I needed. To get to my plate, a fresh vegetable might start in California, travel two thousand miles to Anchorage, travel another two hundred miles to Homer along the highway, then hop the final fifteen miles to Seldovia by boat or plane. Some produce is grown in Alaska, but from our perch beyond the road system, it seems nearly as unreachable as Californian lettuce.

Or I could grow my own. Even I couldn't overspend enough on seeds to set me back more than $150 or so. I didn't see an easy way to avoid shipping bags of flour and rice, but it seemed a little less wasteful not to ship all our lettuce and broccoli as well. It certainly tasted better. No one questioned such a conventional hobby, but with each hand-hauled bucket of water, I thought it was probably best that my enthusiastic endorsements of gardening didn't include a calculation of my time.

There's something intensely satisfying about providing food for myself and my family—growing it, catching it, gathering it, seeing it appear from the very land around me. When the pie is made from berries I've picked, when the salad comes from veggies I've grown, when the fillets come from fish I've caught . . . it's not just food. It feels magical. Maybe it comes from all the time I've spent hungry on expeditions, all the meals I've made of dried food from worn-out ziplock bags, and all the nights I've snuggled into my sleeping bag with a growling ache in my stomach, dreaming of abundance. Maybe it comes from a primal urge to provide for my family. The satisfaction of triumphing over the puzzle of soil nutrition, pests, and climate. A way to putter around outside and claim that it's useful.

In July, we finally reached the season of infinite vegetables and greens, where I could see the dreams from the seed catalog coming to fruition. Mostly. Mixed up between the abundant kale, broccoli, and radishes were the struggling carrots, bolting salad greens, slow peas, and woody turnips. The huge variation in plant size along the length of the kale bed made clear that some of the soil was lacking some important nutrient. But there was food. And there was progress.

Looking over at Katmai, I saw an upended colander, salad greens strewn on the driveway and wilting in the sun, and fistfuls of rocks tossed in among the beets. We moved on, headed with pail and shovel to the sawdust pile by the soon-to-be washhouse.

I almost never turned the handle of our unplumbed faucet anymore, even in the stumble toward morning coffee. After nearly two years, I'd reprogrammed my habits. I moved through all the mundane pieces of life with the same comfortable inattention that most of us do—that nonfunctional sink as noteworthy as a familiar living room couch. Everyone acclimates. Dede stops her van in the rain to climb out and reset the stuck windshield wipers, reaches through the passenger door to avoid the broken handle on the sliding door, and dodges the drip from the ceiling. At times, I've grown used to sharing my sleeping space with wet clothes, hundreds of mosquitoes, or blowing snow.

I don't prioritize comfort. But I like it.

After a year of trips to town for every shower and load of laundry, and uncountable hand-dipped buckets of water, the washhouse was born. Next door to the yurt and nearly on top of our shallow well, the half-built structure stood barely a dozen feet from the tree it once was. From its open frame, I could see the stump. Perched on the stump, I could see the washhouse. Every wooden building was once some conglomeration of pieces of forests from somewhere. Here, the abstraction was gone. Miniature forest became miniature civilization, each step within view of my window.

First there was a spruce tree, shading the path by our door, towering over our cloth-and-sticks roof, bearing the scar it acquired when the driveway was built. We cringed at its every creak, watching the tip flail in every westerly storm, figuring our chances. After a year and a half of wondering, Hig's chainsaw brought it crashing down into the woods instead. The limbs came off first. Firewood. Then Hig chainsawed the trunk into long logs, slowly heaved and nudged into a neat pile by the side of the driveway. A friend brought his mill to take over the yard, its whirring blades drowning out the sounds of birds and passing airplanes, transforming the logs into beams and siding. I gathered the scraps to wall off new garden beds, and Hig claimed several for shelves. The pile of sawdust was carried in pails to feed the compost pile. Other scraps became firewood. The pile of boards was becoming a neat little eight- by twelve-foot cabin. It would have a shower. A sink with a working tap. A washer. A dryer. And best of all, in my current thinking, an outdoor hose that could reach every bed of my garden.

In the picture-perfect version of our Alaskan story, we would have built it ourselves. I might have been a pioneer woman with a hammer in my hand and baby on my back. But I am not that woman. The baby on my back I could handle. But I'm nervous about power tools, impatient with careful measurements, incapable of pounding a nail straight, and generally incompetent in all things construction-related. We hired our friend Chris, who, in addition to running his skiff for halibut and keeping an amazing garden, was actually a carpenter. This step saved us uncounted hours of time. But where were those hours?

I'd spent summers in Alaska before, but this summer was different. This was the first time in my adult life I had a home. Like many young people, I had spent most of my twenties bouncing between dilapidated rentals chosen for their price and proximity to college buildings and bus routes, feeling no connection to their weedy yards, cracked pavement, or peeling paint. When Hig and I walked out on that life to begin our four-thousand-mile journey to the Aleutian Islands, we didn't live anywhere.

But now we did. On the course of that yearlong walk, daydreaming through the blowing snow, we created a new reality. We'd dreamed our way to a home and a child. To a community. To a garden we counted on to feed us, a woodpile we'd count on to warm us, and a half-finished well we needed to make the growing washhouse useful. To a feeling of being rooted, and a long list of chores to do before the snow flies.

Is it possible to be a rooted adventurer? We were planning a month-long expedition at the end of the summer, the longest we'd done since that pivotal journey, and the longest we'd done with a child. I felt a mix of excitement and stress about the whole idea of going. The curiosity, ambition, and craving for adventure that had first sent me into the wilderness pulled me just as strongly as before. But now, home pulled as well. I wanted to go, and to stay. To have a year with more than twelve months, so I could spend one summer gardening, fishing, and gathering, and another summer loose in wild country.

I began to picture our life divided: A third on our feet, in thickets and tundra and villages, exploring the potential and consequences of resource extraction. A third in the mud or snow at the doorstep of the yurt, with all the ordinary chores of life and a few unusual ones besides. And a third in our chairs, pecking away on laptop computers, researching and writing and talking on teleconferences. From that chair, I might be plowing through an environmental impact statement on oil drilling, researching the retreat of glaciers, writing an essay on a visit to a mine or a technical report on discharges from supertankers. And within every one of these juggled lives, I was juggling one blond sprite of a toddler—passing dried pineapple over my shoulder as I ducked beneath alders, sharing water poured all over the driveway and batter mixed all over the counter, and getting up at the tug of a small hand to read yet another truck story.

I wondered how these lives fit together. Hig and I were building up our homestead skills but aching to get back to our own peculiar area of expertise—longing for the singular focus, adventure, and exploration of a real expedition. Could we do it all with a kid in tow? Could stubbornness conquer those seemingly insurmountable logistics? We'd never know without trying. So we settled for a multiple-personality summer, bouncing back and forth between our half-finished projects, half-picked berries, and half-weedy garden to places where the stakes of resource development and climate change are higher and more immediate than our own backyard.

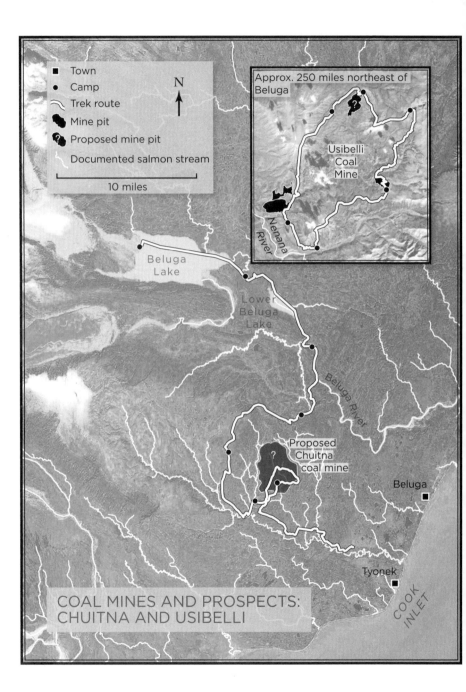

Town
Camp
Trek route
Mine pit
Proposed mine pit
Documented salmon stream

N

10 miles

Approx. 250 miles northeast of Beluga

Usibelli
Coal
Mine

Nenana
River

Beluga
Lake

Lower
Beluga
Lake

Beluga River

Proposed
Chuitna
coal mine
?

Beluga

Tyonek

COOK
INLET

COAL MINES AND PROSPECTS:
CHUITNA AND USIBELLI

PART II

Edges of Alaska

5: Walking on Coal

I WANDERED OUTSIDE Judy and Larry's cabin, admiring the young lettuces and cabbages in Judy's gardens—easily ahead of my own—while Katmai stood with his face squashed into the wire mesh of the chicken yard, absorbed in the strutting and squawking. Their hand-built log house was one of only a handful of structures in the small community of Beluga, home to a few dozen people on the west side of Cook Inlet. With Anchorage at its head and the somewhat populated Kenai Peninsula forming its southeastern border, the east side of Cook Inlet is home to hundreds of thousands of people. Between Beluga and the nearby Native village of Tyonek, the west side is home to just hundreds—living with moose, salmon, volcanoes, and hydrocarbons.

Beluga was a boat ride, shuttle van, and small plane flight away—120 miles from Seldovia. It was the beginning of an eight-day journey, more than we'd ever done as parents. It was the first step toward a monthlong trip we weren't quite sure was possible with a kid. Beluga was a memory from a snowy February two years ago; skis squealing through the dark on a sharp crust of ice, meeting Judy and Larry in the warm bubble of this cabin. It was also a place to touch an issue that had been burrowing questions in my mind since we'd first set foot in this spot.

Erin and Katmai walk the edge of a beaver dam in the Chuitna Coal prospect.

In the Cook Inlet basin, pools of oil and gas saturate layers of folded sediments. Oil rigs have stood here since the 1950s, decades before oil was discovered on Alaska's North Slope. Natural gas from Cook Inlet supplies energy to most of the people in the state—much of it running through the screeching hulk of a power plant that is Beluga's reason for existence. But there's coal here too, newly reborn into the dreams of mining companies as Asia's coal consumption grows. Beluga stands beside the Chuitna River, in the shadow of the proposed Chuitna Coal Mine—an eight-square-mile pit that could exhume one tiny sliver of the four trillion tons of coal beneath Alaskan soil.

On any journey, we learn about ourselves and so much more—a hundred more important things about the world beyond our own emotions. It was a revelation that grew to become our mission: Go out and see, touch, smell, talk to people, take pictures, and write everything down. Come back and share it, seeking to touch on crucial and sometimes forgotten issues by sharing those stories, those facts, and our many hours of background research, with the peculiar twist of perspective that comes from being at the ground truth of things.

Hig and I wrote our summer plans as a tidy, coal-themed arc. From Chuitna, we would travel to Usibelli, Alaska's only operating coal mine, and then to the vast coal deposits in the Arctic—exploring the future of the fuel that nobody associated with Alaska. Those four trillion tons of coal that might, or might not, reshape our world.

⌘

The bear showed up on our first day out. We were barely beyond the road, still following the ruts of a four-wheeler track, inching along at a pace that never let us outdistance June's cloud of mosquitoes. Katmai toddled uncertainly ahead of me, and I watched the ground at his feet, gently directing him back to the trail when his legs or attention strayed. Until I glanced up to a shadow of black. The familiar sauntering shape slid behind an alder bush, then peered out from behind the next one. First I grabbed Katmai, then Hig and I each grabbed our pepper spray, confronting the bear in our best low-pitched and disapproving voices. My "bad dog" voice.

Unlike the keychain versions sold to nervous city dwellers, pepper spray for bears comes in canisters the size of shampoo bottles, with holsters designed to attach to the strap of a pack. Pull the safety, squeeze the trigger, and a charging bear gets a cloud of stinging pepper in mouth and nose. Statistics show it to be a better defense than a gun. But in hundreds of encounters, we've never needed to use any defense at all. Of the things that scare people about the wilderness, bears often top the list. Of the things that actually hurt them, bears run far behind steep slopes, fast water, and the chill of hypothermia.

I clutched Katmai's wiggling body to my hip as he squealed and pointed at the bear, hugging himself in an enthusiastic version of the "bear" sign, as if he wished nothing more than to run and meet this hero of toddler literature. I had taught him bits and pieces of sign language, and he now had dozens of crude representations of animal signs to round out his small vocabulary.

The bear left, but an hour later, it reappeared, skulking in the bushes a little ways behind us. We yelled. Then it was gone again. It never confronted us. Never threatened to charge. As bear encounters go, it was far less intense and frightening than many others I've had over the years. But this bear *followed* us, and that was new for me. It was inescapably creepy. I could only guess the bear was really following Katmai, hoping the vulnerable young one might be left unattended. I shuddered at the thought. Katmai didn't just change our tolerance for risk—he changed the risk itself. Was this trip even a good idea?

Hig and I had never stopped doing short trips, but this was our first full-on backpacking trip with a walking, talking, exploring toddler. Everything was harder. From analyzing and mitigating the risks of wilderness travel, to keeping everyone happy and warm and fed, to the logistics of carrying our gear, to dealing with diapers in the field, to having enough time and energy to focus on what had brought us to this patch of wild ground in the first place.

I didn't need to come all the way out here to say that a coal mine will be uglier than a meadow. That this chunk of wilderness is more beautiful and wild, less polluted, and more full of life than it would be as a coal mine. Of course that's true. And not just for coal mines, but for wind turbines, factories, cities full of people, and nearly anything humans might do to the land. But it's harder to argue for coal mines. The coal—destined for export from a state that already produces more than it can use—won't bring cheaper energy. Any industry requires workers, but coal—measured in investment dollars per jobs produced—is one of the least effective ways to create them. The couple hundred local people, despite their current lack of economic opportunities, are some of the strongest opponents of the mine.

Judy and Larry pictured coal dust wafting over their homes and dead salmon in their rivers. But it wouldn't stop there. A mine here would snake its influence far beyond this unknown chunk of land, reaching out like pea-vine tendrils to grasp onto every one of us. Coal mined is coal burned. Releasing brain-damaging mercury, forest- and lung-damaging nitrous oxide and sulfur dioxide, and world-damaging carbon dioxide. Since the industrial revolution, we've been burning chains of carbon that were trapped beneath the earth for millions of years as oil, gas, and coal. These are fossil fuels, brought back to life, filling the atmosphere with carbon dioxide molecules that trap more of the sun's heat. We measure them in parts per million; around 280 in 1800, around 315 in 1950, and more than 390 parts per million today, spreading around the globe to impact everyone. Small-sounding numbers that send global temperature upward, where just a scant few degrees can bring sea-level rise, storms, droughts, and a hundred other painful consequences. This is why the islands near Seldovia are gray with beetle-killed trees. This is why we could bring my mother to walk on rocks where glaciers used to be.

Coal's chemical structure means that burning it creates even more carbon dioxide per unit of energy than other fossil fuels. Its abundance in the earth means that the difference between a future where we burn it freely—Alaska's four trillion tons of coal and many trillions of tons more—and one where we don't, is a stark and frightening difference. Reclaiming the site of a coal mine is difficult. We may never be able to bring salmon streams and wetlands back to the way they used to be. Bringing the world back—to the one we grew up in—is truly impossible.

Coal boulders poked above the churning brown waters of the Chuitna River, while shining ribbons of coal seams followed the curving banks.

"What if we name the baby after somewhere on the Lost Coast?" I mused, fingering a shiny black pebble.

"Um, sure," Hig replied. "Can we talk about that later? Can you think of a good way to photograph that coal seam on the far side?"

I couldn't. But I took the camera anyway, snapping a few shots while continuing to daydream about baby names.

Just before we set out on this monthlong trip, we had been surprised to learn that I was nearly three months pregnant with our second child. And while my current child was sleeping, my thoughts drifted to the next one.

Katmai was named for a volcano protruding through an otherworldly landscape of twisted canyons and fused volcanic ash—the site of the twentieth century's largest eruption—ringed by the vast wild green of Katmai National Park. We'd fallen in love with it nearly a decade before his birth. I needed a name just as special for the next baby. The Lost Coast is a remote stretch of battered beaches and garnet sand on the Gulf of Alaska, where wild storms alternate with gorgeous sunsets, ice fills the few bays, and massive glaciers reach up to towering snowcapped peaks. Something there should fit.

We hadn't yet told a soul about this fourth expedition member. The wild hormones of pregnancy left me snappy, crankier than usual, and sometimes exhausted while Katmai was awake. I was excited to welcome another child, but we were only just figuring out how to adventure as a family of three. How on earth would I manage to add one more logistical burden to the mix?

Hig's backpack was a misshapen monster in black ripstop nylon, already stuffed beyond its cinch-string top with everything from paddle blades to cheese to diapers. As I walked behind him, a bulging pouch of food thumped gently on my chest with every step, suspended by the straps of the wrap that held Katmai to my back, who was resting above the jumbo-sized fanny pack that carried more food and water bottles. I felt like a well-decorated Christmas tree.

Katmai rode in a wrap like he did as a baby, only now on my back. With his head just behind my shoulder, I could protect both of our faces from marauding branches. My overlarge raincoat had a slit for his head to poke through, bug netting to pull up over him, and a girth I hoped would be sufficient for both my toddler and my growing belly. Katmai was light for his age. He still felt heavy.

Most of our planning for this trip had focused on one essential question: How much could we carry? Which really meant: How far could we go? When it was just the two of us, we managed to travel two weeks between food resupplies, whittling down our gear weight, and cramming our packs with cheese, pasta, butter, and chocolate. We slept in a one-pound floorless tent. When it was cold, we wore every stitch of clothing we had with us, except for one dry pair of socks saved for bedtime. We shared a sleeping bag, pot, spoon, and toothbrush. We forded streams in our soaking-wet trail-running shoes. We ate the highest calorie food we could get away with, and when our estimates turned out to be wrong, we went hungry. When we had to—when we wanted to go where no one was—we sometimes crossed hundreds of miles before reaching another settlement.

We still did all of that. All but the hundreds of miles at a stretch. All but the hunger. At twenty pounds, Katmai's weight was the equivalent of about five days of food. So instead of fourteen days of food, we might be able to carry nine. But the extra clothes and diapers we had to bring for him weighed something too. With both a toddler and unborn child depending on us, we needed more food per day and couldn't risk running out. And Katmai was more than just a sack of flour—he was a sack of flour that needed time to sit in the mud and explore the meadows in meandering circles, drastically reducing our daily mileage. This meant that we needed to carry more food to cover the same amount of terrain.

How far could we go? Maybe eight miles a day? And how hard would those eight miles be? Could we carry more since we were walking fewer miles? Could we manage an eight-day trip? In our long evenings of planning, my spreadsheet of ounces and pounds glowed back at me from the computer screen, silently failing to answer any of my actual questions.

We left the river for the mine site. The coal was invisible again, buried deep beneath a patchwork of grassy meadows, beaver ponds, birch woods, and wetlands. In mining parlance, ours was a journey on the "overburden"—the stuff that sits on top of the stuff the coal company wants to mine. If the mine is built, the meadow and soil beneath my feet would be scraped down to rock, then the rock itself would be removed, tossed aside until all that is left is a seam of coal within the rubble. With each step, I might have pictured that future.

Instead, I listened to the roar of beaver-engineered waterfalls, the squelch of our footsteps on living peat, and the ever-present drone of mosquitoes. We swished through feathery ostrich ferns, clambered through thickets of highbush cranberry, and breathed wafts of fragrant sweet gale. The green of June was eye-popping. Climbing, my heavy breathing reminded me of the ponderous slowness that creeps into pregnancy. The landscape reminded me of a savannah, and I pulled out the camera, trying to frame a lone birch against the sky.

Every time we set out on a journey, I learn things. But the things I learn aren't always what I expect or plan for. We were here to live a story about a coal mine. But at that moment, abstract thoughts about local pollution and global climate change quickly faded in the vibrancy of that savannah in the sun. Whatever vision had led us there, the journey, like any journey, was about the place itself.

Katmai stirred, pushing aside my dreamy philosophizing with a cranky, not-quite-awake squawk. I reached over my shoulder, handing him a cracker for one fist and a long blade of grass for the other. Most of the time, I carried on two conversations at once—discussing plans and landscape with Hig, while keeping up a patter of toddler-level commentary on our surroundings, responding to an array of poorly articulated sounds and vague sign language.

ME [POINTING]: "So that's the big fault up on Lone Ridge. It really stands out, doesn't it?"

HIG: "Yep. It's a section of the Lake Clark Fault—the same one that runs by Pebble Mine off to the west."

KATMAI: "Dihdo Boom!"

ME: "Yes, that is a big stump. Do you see the trees?"

HIG: "See that tree that fell down in a *big* wind? The fault runs for around 150 miles, but this is the only place where you can actually see it. I'm not sure exactly why that is."

ME: "Look, Katmai, another beaver dam, and a little waterfall coming off it. Is this depression we're walking in part of the fault?"

KATMAI [SIGNING "WATER"]

HIG: "Yes, that's water flowing. This sort of slump is called a graben—it's probably part of the fault."

ME [PASSING KATMAI A LEAF]: "These are alder bushes. They have lots of green leaves."

KATMAI [IMMEDIATELY DROPPING THE LEAF]: "Moh? Moh?"

Eventually the conversations would devolve into screaming, soon accompanied by my off-key singing of nursery rhymes, and finally end in a hasty unwrapping, a tumble of piled-up gear, and a rustling diaper bag. Katmai would beeline for my lap, latching on to nurse in eager desperation, as if I'd been away for weeks, then suddenly bound away as if I didn't exist at all. He charged across the landscape with a toddler-sized walking stick, leaving zigzags, loops, and circles in rows of bowlegged footprints.

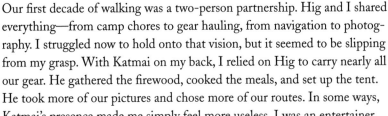

Our first decade of walking was a two-person partnership. Hig and I shared everything—from camp chores to gear hauling, from navigation to photography. I struggled now to hold onto that vision, but it seemed to be slipping from my grasp. With Katmai on my back, I relied on Hig to carry nearly all our gear. He gathered the firewood, cooked the meals, and set up the tent. He took more of our pictures and chose more of our routes. In some ways, Katmai's presence made me simply feel more useless. I was an entertainer, snack fixer, sippy cup filler, and poison plant watcher. But was I still an adventurer?

Drawn into toddler world, I did my best to embrace it. Katmai knew nothing of the complicated plans and goals and worries and self-image that shaped my own expectations. He was solidly anchored in the physical world—the present moment. It's a cliché that a kid can play for hours with a stick in the dirt. But as I struggled to curb my impatience to crest the next hill, I was forced to admit the cliché was true.

I've taken my share of photos of flowers and bugs over the years. But I've also always been a big-picture planner, dreaming up more and more ambitious journeys, half my brain always tuned to some larger goal. Toddler zen is not my natural frame of mind. With Katmai, I found myself sucked into something smaller and muddier, less goal-driven and more immediate than any journey before. Who says a seagull isn't exciting? Couldn't all of us use some toddler eyes?

I dove into a thicket of highbush cranberry bushes, moving at an even-slower-than-usual pace as I waited for Katmai to notice each bunch of last year's wrinkled dry fruit, and then angled my shoulder so he could reach out and grab them.

～

Toddler zen was not going to get us to our pick-up point at the end of the week. The first day's bear encounter was fading in my mind, replaced by the day-to-day difficulties of actually getting as far as we meant to. The brush was thicker than we'd hoped. The toddler, slower and more demanding. Our plan to raft down the Beluga River then loop back up alongside it in a ten-mile bushwhack looked rather more daunting than it had on a computer screen.

Increasingly, my worries turned to the water waiting ahead of us. Alaska is crisscrossed by wild rivers—cold, fast, and opaque with glacial silt—spilling out of icefields and snowcapped mountains, rushing dozens or hundreds of miles without a dam or bridge. They present one of the most formidable obstacles to wilderness travel. A few brave souls swim them, but most use packrafts.

The sport of packrafting is a staple of Alaska backcountry adventure. Backpackers carry small inflatable rafts, four or five pounds each, and multipart kayak paddles. In a pack, one raft is about the size of a large chunk of firewood. At the water's edge, the boat is unrolled and inflated with the help of a simple bag with a nozzle on one end, ballooning into a bright rubber oval that's only five feet long but sturdy enough for wilderness whitewater. The paddler sits on a blow-up seat on a fabric floor, surrounded by an inflated tube, in a craft resembling a tiny snub-nosed kayak. Then the pack is strapped onto the boat that was once in the pack, completing the traveler's amphibious transformation. After eight years of using packrafts, I knew how it might perform in the water. I didn't want to find out how the baby would.

A day and a half before we hit the Beluga River, I was already starting to second-guess our plan. "I'm worried about floating the Beluga with Katmai—I don't want to take him into any rapids."

"It's okay—the river is really mellow, with lots of sandbars and beaches," Hig proclaimed with a nonchalant confidence. "Even if there is a rapid, it should be easy to walk around."

As the river got closer, I spent more time staring at its curves on the map, disbelief edging me into a more fervent discussion. "Are you sure about the river? Because that section looks pretty constricted on the map."

"I looked at it on Google Earth. And remember the Iskut River?" Hig commented, bringing us back to a distant gorge we'd rafted through three years earlier and over seven hundred miles away. "You can have a narrow section and still have a mellow river with lots of gravel bars."

A few hours from the river, I wouldn't let the subject drop. "It really does look like a gorge here. And I know there are gorges without rapids, but both Larry and the pilot at Felt Lake said there *was* a gorge with big rapids on this river."

"They both said the gorge was much closer to the Beluga Lakes—well upstream of where we're planning to float." In one form or another, we always have this debate. Hig with the rosy view, and me with my doubts. He calls me the Voice of Reason, the one who keeps our plans in line with reality. An incorrigible devil's advocate, I am the one who pokes holes in every plan before we work together to patch them, spews out a flurry of problems before I turn to the solutions, turning each idea upside down and shaking it until I'm sure it's watertight.

The Beluga River greeted us with an ominous roar—a wide expanse of milky brown tumbling downstream into churning waves. A rapid boiled just downstream, before the river turned a corner, out of sight. We ate spaghetti on the river bar, trying to keep Katmai's sandy fingers out of the pot, searching for a plan B.

Poring over the map, Hig admitted that he hadn't ever looked at *this* stretch of river on Google Earth—he'd looked much farther downstream. I could have said "I told you so." Instead, we both laughed. Our discussion wasn't based in anger. And it wasn't avoidable—the analysis and arguments of these debates were as critical to our expeditions as editing is to writing. From them, we can claim more than a decade of safe adventure—no injuries for either one of us beyond a blister or scrape.

Our pickup point was actually upstream, along water we could now see was smooth. The downstream loop we had planned would let us visit another coal prospect, but it was expendable. Hig struggled to paddle our 350 pounds of people and gear upstream in a current that was less sluggish than it looked, while I filled bags with sticks and rocks as toddler toys, keeping a firm grasp on Katmai's wiggly torso as he threw them into the river. At Beluga Lake, Mount Spurr towered just inland of our campsite on a blanket of volcanic cinders. We spent two nights in the same campsite, relaxing into the novelty of relaxation itself. When we flew out the next day, we branded the trip a success.

I wasn't sure what we'd succeeded at. Staying alive and mostly happy? Yes. Making it to our pickup point without running out of food or diapers? Yes. Gaining a greater understanding of the potential coal mine? Maybe. Having the best possible adventure with a toddler? Probably not. Having some impact on the issue of coal development? Only time could tell.

In any case, we didn't have a lot of time to worry about it. In only eight days, our coal-themed arc would draw us onward to the next piece of our adventure: Usibelli. There we'd have our only chance to visit an actual coal mine. Between the whirlwind of flying home, and then boating and driving more than four hundred miles to Usibelli, there wasn't much time to reflect and prepare. Some of our gear already needed repair; we hoped we would have time to repair it. Our system had basically worked; we hoped it would work again.

⌒⁄⌒

Deep in the interior of the state, near Denali National Park, Usibelli looked more like Utah than the Alaska I knew. We approached the mine through a twisting canyon, where soft rock sculpted into wavy ridges and improbable spires, with spruce trees and wildflowers perching on their peaks. Stripes of shiny black coal stood out against the light gray and brown of the surrounding rocks, shifting to brick red where the coal seams had burned underground. Rain squalls blew over us. A giant earthmover swung slowly back and forth in the distance, gleaming yellow-orange against the gray-black pit.

"Hey Katmai! Look at the *very big* machine!"

"Aren't rainbows supposed to point to gold?" Hig quipped, pointing to the shimmering arc touching down in one of Usibelli's recently abandoned mine pits.

"Let's go catch it, then. See if they missed something."

Perhaps we should have gone here first, setting our boots to this real open-pit coal mine before trying to visualize one at Chuitna. But Alaska is too big and too diverse to draw easy parallels. I couldn't imagine a more different ecosystem from Chuitna. Instead of beaver dams, marshes, and grassy birch savannahs, here there were tundra ridges of wildflowers and forests of slender cone-shaped spruce. Instead of lush green, we walked through tawny yellow. Instead of swatting mosquitoes, we suffered through the heat.

Ribbons of coal striped the pale sandstone bluffs. A fledging great horned owl perched on a gleaming black slash, watching us nervously. At Chuitna, we had hoped to tell the story of coal in Alaska. But while we had traveled on the "overburden" of marshes and meadows, we had barely glimpsed the coal. Here it was everywhere—in the mine pits and all around them—so bold in its presence that I needed neither maps nor geologists to point it out. Coal-streaked hillsides were punctuated by carved-out pits, where gullies were eroding deep furrows into mountains of left-behind gray. Grass mix grew on planted slopes, followed by patches of scrubby willow and alders.

I have some of that grass mix. We took the official tour of Usibelli Coal Mine, craning our necks to stare at the towering dump trucks, collecting intriguing numbers and facts, listening with skeptical politeness to the enthusiastic PR of the young tour guide. I tossed all of their brochures, including a coloring book for kids. But the packets of reclamation-mix grass are still sitting on my shelf. I've thought of scattering it on the barren gravel on top of our well, but something always holds me back.

Eventually trees will grow in those resculpted mine pits, spruce forests replacing silty gullies. But I suspect that even a hundred years from now, the outlines of the mines will be obvious.

Does that matter? Alaska still has a wealth of remote and wild country. Even today—even as wrong as this idea has been in the world's other wild places—it's easy to imagine that there will always be another valley. In this patch of the state, discolored streams and eroding gullies were the norm before the miners even showed up. But coal is dug to be burned, and that burning always matters. In the carbon dioxide swirling into the atmosphere, and the melting Arctic villages we were soon to visit.

We left Usibelli to retrace two days of driving, in a friend's car, then my mom's, through Anchorage, to Homer, and then the final boat ride to Seldovia. I felt tired. I was ready to get back to my garden, eat fish, and watch the berries ripen. But I felt a little better about expeditions with Katmai. It was possible. It could even be fun. And both Chuitna and Usibelli were short-and-mild preparations for the expedition we'd embark on in a month and a half—the one that had really captured our hearts and imagination: a month on the thawing coast of the Northwest Arctic, where the vast majority of Alaska's coal lies beneath the tundra.

6: The Chukchi Sea at Toddler Speed

THE BROKEN REMAINS of speckled blue eggshells were scattered among the rocks. I pointed them out to Katmai as we walked, every sentence punctuated by the screams of thousands of kittiwakes and murres. An acrid smell wafted off the cliffs below us, and the lush grass on our ridge spoke to a liberal application of bird-derived fertilizer.

Shifting fog opened windows onto the sheer drop-off below, where clusters of birds were plastered on every crack and ledge, turning the craggy rocks into a writhing mass of black and white. They turned wheeling circles above the water, where the Chukchi Sea crashed gray-blue against the cliffs of Cape Lisburne. Marmots burrowed into crevices between the boulders, adding their distinctive whistles to the chorus of the birds. A steep trail cut an angled line across the scree on the far side of the valley, where a half-dozen Dall sheep followed each other over the ridge. Just out of sight, Hig and Katmai were setting up the tent.

"Go in a tent! Go in a tent!"

"Soon! We need to set it up first. Want to help me pull this string?"

It was the middle of August. We were a day and a half into a month-long trek along the remote Chukchi Sea coast in the Northwest Arctic. We

Katmai walks a narrow spit on the shore of an Arctic lagoon.

were well north of the Arctic Circle and nearly eight hundred miles from home—one boat ride and three plane flights before we could even start walking. With an eighteen-month-old. As a five-months-pregnant woman.

⚬⁄⚬

Beneath our steep grassy slope a brown bear lumbered beside a trickle of a stream. He was far away and heading still farther, unaware of our presence. Almost unconsciously, my fingers wormed into my pocket, touching the cool metal canister of pepper spray. I was nowhere close to needing it, but I needed to reassure myself that it was there.

Most fears shrink with familiarity. Whitecapping waves on an ocean bay, swirling eddies on a glacial river, a steep and rocky scramble. But despite years of traveling in grizzly country, my worry over bears only loomed larger with each journey. Every trip out, we see a few more bears. Or a lot more bears. More bears that run away from us as though hikers in grubby raingear are the most terrifying thing they've ever seen. More bears ambling along in pursuit of berries, never even noticing us. But also more bears charging toward us, sizing us up, sending my heart thumping into my throat. Each terrifyingly close encounter lodges in my mind more firmly than the multitude of innocuous sightings. And having Katmai along put all my protective instincts into overdrive.

As soon as we set foot on the Arctic shore, we were in the realm of the bears. Bear tracks stepped upon bear tracks, weaving back and forth across the smudged depressions left by older bear tracks. There were paths beaten down by the bears at the top of the beach, in the middle of the beach, and vanishing into the lapping waves. Their trails crisscrossed around a dead whale washed up on shore, where they had feasted on the rotting flesh. Nestlike depressions in the sand marked where they had slept off their meals. Katmai toddled—a half-dozen steps for every one of the bears'—as my eyes scanned the horizon in either direction, squinting for the hint of a dark moving shape.

Our first lunch break brought our first flesh-and-blood bear. Katmai and I filled water bottles at a creek while Hig gathered wood for a fire. The bear spray cans sat in their instantly grabbable chest pouches—which we'd left next to the packs, a handful of steps behind Hig. Then we saw it, rounding a rare blind corner in the open terrain, and almost on top of our campfire. It saw us, but not the kid. Katmai didn't notice it either, busy throwing pebbles into the creek with a backdrop of squeaky chatter that now seemed cringingly loud.

We both knew the rules. You shouldn't ever run from a bear—potentially triggering a predatory chase. You also would do better to be holding some sort of deterrent—that bear spray we'd left by the packs. Hig went for the spray, backing up in a hasty rush he hoped appeared like anything but a run. The bear lurched forward in the wake of Hig's retreat, but hesitated when he spun around to face off with it, spray in hand. I moved to stand between Katmai and the bear, too far away to do anything but watch.

The bear was likely just a few years old—an ursine teenager—testing its limits. Such bears can often be bluffed into submission. This one fit the pattern, stomping aggressively to see if we'd run, then galloping away when Hig advanced instead. It circled around to see if we really meant it, looking for a tactical advantage from a perch on the small dunes above us. Hig was there to meet it, charging up with pepper spray in hand. That was enough. The bear beat a hasty retreat—fleeing down the beach, its bounding rump vanishing into the distance. I filed the encounter in my extensive mental catalog of normal bear behavior. We finished our lunch, and continued, on top of bear tracks, down the beach.

It had worked out the way that things almost always do; appropriate human behavior, appropriate bear behavior, and no need to even use the defense we carried. But after that, the pepper spray traveled with us at every moment—through day and night, on rest breaks and berry-picking stops and water-filling excursions. After that, we ate our meals where we had a long view of *all* the terrain around us, keeping half an eye on the horizon.

Hig and I have always prided ourselves on a cool-headed analysis of risk and the overall safety record of our journeys. If we weren't endangering ourselves in the first place, did being parents really change anything? But it wasn't just the bears. I knew that a child being carried wouldn't keep warm as well as a walking adult could. Katmai wouldn't know how to keep moving to stave off hypothermia in dangerous weather. A packraft-flipping wave would leave him reliant on the small orange comfort of his life vest. Fully dependent on our wisdom, in every circumstance.

Despite all the careful planning we'd done to mitigate every one of the potential hazards, when I listened to the steady sleeping breaths on my back, I felt the weight of his vulnerability as well as that of the unborn child inside me.

◦◦◦

Hig and Katmai had finished their tent project. Closed off from the view now, we lay in our sleeping bag, listening to marmot whistles and bird calls through the nylon walls. Whatever the environment, some things about parenting never change. Like *sleep*. When parents of young children meet, the discussion inevitably turns to the exasperating and ridiculous difficulty of such a basic bodily function.

Katmai crawled in and out of bed, bounced on top of us, clomped over our gear in Daddy's shoes, snuggled up for a quick nursing session, and then wriggled out again, seemingly inexhaustible. We lay there for hours, eyes half closed in hopefulness. Finally, he crashed. Beyond exhausted myself, I rolled over to sleep in the tight quarters of our homemade three-person sleeping bag, trying to ignore the slowly increasing wind.

The shuddering of our tent gave way to a booming thunder, as the walls billowed and slapped with every gust. Stretched taut and strummed like the strings of an out-of-tune guitar, the cords that held our home to earth worked back and forth over the sharp edges of the rocks that weighed them down. Knives make poor tent stakes. Suddenly, several of the ties snapped, releasing the tent into a flying tangle of advanced geometry. I crouched over Katmai as a human shield, attempting to keep the nylon from pummeling him awake. Hig crawled out of the tent, naked and barefoot in the driving mist, retying the frazzled ends of the strings until we had something over our heads again.

Spooked by the bears, we'd camped in the most out-of-the-way place we could find. Cliffs dropped down on two sides, where our narrow ridge abruptly fell away into the Chukchi Sea. Nothing but us to break the storms.

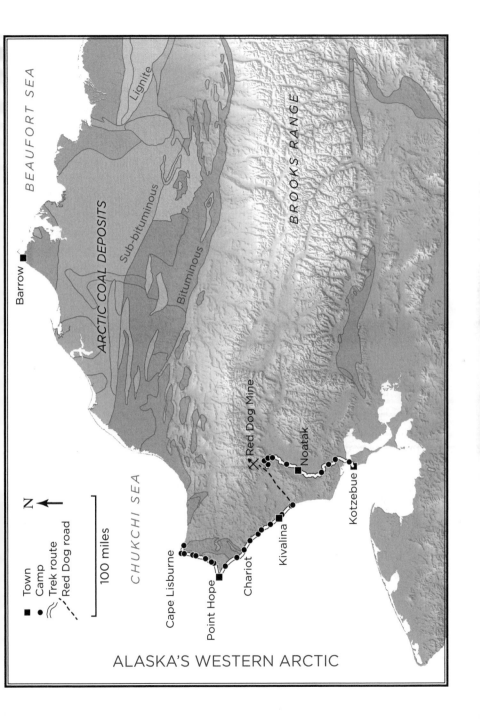

ALASKA'S WESTERN ARCTIC

BEAUFORT SEA

Barrow

Lignite

ARCTIC COAL DEPOSITS

Sub-bituminous

Bituminous

BROOKS RANGE

Red Dog Mine

Noatak

Kotzebue

CHUKCHI SEA

N

100 miles

■ Town
● Camp
〰 Trek route
--- Red Dog road

Cape Lisburne

Point Hope

Chariot

Kivalina

The wind rose, and we repeated the process over and over again, until we were crouched in a strange small shape that barely resembled our original pyramid. Hig experimented with different ways of tying the tent, eventually swapping the paddle pole out for a shorter walking stick, and adding a long line that ran out directly into the wind. We hunkered in the one small bubble of space remaining, as the cacophony of our flapping walls blended with the cacophony of the world around us.

Midway through the night, Katmai's rainpants were sucked out of the tent, vanishing into the Arctic night, perhaps fluttering down to the Chukchi Sea seven hundred feet below us. He slept soundly between us as we yelled back and forth about our lack of options.

"Should we move?!" I called out.

"Move where?!"

"I don't know, but we'll never get to sleep like this!"

"By the time we find a new spot, it'll be morning anyway!"

Hig was right. Unless we were prepared to pack up and walk for miles in search of a tuck-in away from both wind and bears, there was nowhere else to sleep and no sleep to be had. Falling into an exhausted silence, I stared out at the wind-whipped grass under the flapping edge of the tent, watching black turn to gray as the world slowly lightened—waiting for morning.

I made my way down to the beach the next morning in a grumpy fog of tiredness, wondering what we might have done differently. We were only two days into a monthlong adventure, and already we'd experienced the swirling exhilaration of the rookeries, of wildlife and sunsets and pictur-esque fog, and the bright face of a toddler seeing his first wild sheep. We'd also faced moments of terror in the standoff with the bear, and a long and sleepless night in a storm—stereotypical manifestations of the tired old "man against nature" theme.

"Does adventure always have to be uncomfortable?" I grumbled. "No matter how much we learn, we always seem to end up cold, wet, tired, or hungry. Is that just a risk we accept along the way—or is it the adventure itself?"

"I think people try too hard to be comfortable," Hig replied. "You gain a lot by being tolerant of discomfort."

"But it goes the other way too," I offered. "Back when we were just starting out, we had an amazing trip with that crappy little tarp and the leaky rafts that made us soaked all the time. We travel so much more comfortably now—most of the time—and I don't see that we've lost anything from it."

"Sure, but that kind of misses the point. We still push our own limits. And there's so much we would lose if we didn't do that anymore."

"Of course. If I didn't want to push limits, I never would have suggested that we could come out here and do this with a kid—or while pregnant. But we *can* choose smarter campsites." We'd had this discussion before, and we followed a well-worn path of memorized arguments as we picked our way down a slippery slope of rocks and grass. It seems to push us back into stereotypes: the stoic mountain man and his wife who just wants to be warm.

There *is* something to be gained by being uncomfortable. Small discomforts are easily skated over by the force of habit. Putting on wet socks each morning and wearing them through ice-cold streams. Crawling out of a warm sleeping bag into a frigid morning. Walking through tiredness. Walking through darkness. Walking through rain. All the things that are an inevitable part of how we travel through wild country. With dry feet, I would have seen a lot less of the world than I have today.

But most of the larger discomforts we've experienced over the years are more easily classified as "mistakes." Different gear, a wiser route choice, a more generous food calculation, a better reading of the water or the weather. In avoiding the bears, we'd placed ourselves high on the ridges of Cape Lisburne, with no protection at all from the weather. An easy mistake to make on a calm day. An easy mistake to avoid tomorrow. On our earlier yearlong journey, we could have calculated our food more accurately—seeing the wilderness without being forced to live off Betty Crocker frosting or peppermints or our own fat reserves. We could have seen it without going snow-blind or being buried in a snow drift, or having our tent destroyed by a bear. But all of that happened. And it will happen again—different only in detail.

We learn from our errors. The gear we carry today is light-years ahead of what we lugged ten years ago, in weight, comfort, and function. In how it can flex to help us adapt to the unexpected. Our skills have improved similarly. But errors that seem idiotic in hindsight are still embarrassingly frequent. Perhaps this is the crux of what it means to be serial adventurers. Each time we learn more. But what we learn is never enough. We push back to the edge of incompetence, seeking our space between the epically miserable and the simply routine. There is always a complication. This time, it was a toddler.

∽

Grasping the ends of the long piece of cloth, I tied it into a snug knot above my bulging pregnant belly. From his half-secured perch on my bent-over back, Katmai grabbed the hat off my head, gleefully tossing it onto the ground. Knots finished, hat retrieved, hiking commenced. I pulled out a sippy cup of powdered milk mixed with water—hoping to occupy his hands as much as quench his thirst.

We stopped an hour later. We'd figured out the rhythm by now, figured out that all our sweaty efforts as beasts of burden must be balanced out, for the sake of the kid, with periods of blissful laziness. While I rested my feet in the sand, Katmai clomped around enthusiastically in my shoes. He tripped, stumbled out of the giant-sized sneakers, and sprinted toward the beach in a toddler's wobbly gait. He threw rocks. He waded in the trickles that ran down the beach, and threw ptarmigan feathers into the wind. We sat while he moved and walked while he rode—seesawing roles that took nearly equal chunks of time. Walk, look, pause, play, walk, look, pause, play, walk . . . .

A flock of kittiwakes wheeled overhead, squeaking and crying before landing in the ocean. Hig shrugged his shoulders and adjusted the straps of his overloaded pack. I watched the orange and purple forms of tiny washed-up sea stars, wondering how so many had ended up dead—and where was the evidence of their prey? Sunset shimmered yellow on the glassy calm sea.

"I see buuu twash!" Katmai crowed with excitement. "Buu twash bad?"

Right. A dark blue bottle with faded lettering, maybe for motor oil, in the drift of sticks and sea stars. "Yes, Katmai, blue trash is bad."

"Gweeen twash! Big gweeen twash! Gweeen twash bad!"

I acknowledged the rusting green oil drum, and tried to turn his attention instead to the caribou rib cage protruding above the sand, surrounded by the fleshy yellowing stalks of beach greens. Without Katmai, I was quite successfully ignoring the trash—as common as bones. There was less of it here than on many coasts I've walked. But everywhere the ocean touches, plastic water bottles and fishing buoys wash ashore, interspersed with colorful flotsam of a hundred other descriptions.

Walking across the wilderness, the immediate layer we see is the present moment. We see one beach only in a rainstorm—the next beach only in the sun. But the more we learn, the more we can pick out shadows of the past, and premonitions of the future.

On top of a mountain at Cape Lisburne, there stands a house-sized geodesic dome. We approached it in a thick fog, which when combined with shadowy figures spraying the walls in full-body hazmat suits, made me feel this was a sort of sci-fi movie I'd rather not be in. Noting my own lack of a hazmat suit, and my role as the bearer of two vulnerable children, I hurried past without pausing to find out what was being sprayed, staying upwind. Hig stopped to talk, but only for a moment.

In that moment he found out that the dome is for radar. In the 1950s it was just one piece of a remote Air Force base, on the frontlines of the Cold War. Now, barracks and scattered buildings topple back into the tundra. A few contractors keep the radar working, still scanning the sky for planes and missiles. Over seven hundred miles northwest of Anchorage, and thousands of miles from the rest of highways-and-cities-America, it's easy to think of this coast as far from everything. But America once knew it best for being close to Russia. A mere two hundred miles to the west, old Soviet military installations stare across the gap from their own tundra wilderness.

Visible from nearly everywhere in this treeless terrain, the garish white dome is the latest addition to the long history of humans in the Arctic. Villages on the Chukchi Sea stretch back hundreds or even thousands of years, from clusters of new wooden buildings to the subtle depressions of ancient house pits. At a glance, it looks too barren for humans. The hills are rubble, vegetation nothing but a patchy green scum on their surface, petering out entirely only a few hundred feet above the sea. Even the beaches seem oddly empty, lacking the familiar detritus of mussel-covered rocks, barnacles, and ribbons of seaweed. In the winter, ice grinds along this narrow waterline, killing anything in its path.

But the coast is made of bones. Caribou ribs. Fish vertebrae. Whale skulls stand on the beach—waist-high boulders with gaping eye holes—like ghosts looking over the sea. Bone fragments crumble from the bluffs where houses once clustered—discards from a million human meals. The bones showed us the richness hidden beneath the Chukchi Sea. We could see it also in the cliffs spattered with bird guano and in the bear-torn flesh of a washed-up seal. Ice edge algal blooms begin a cascade of life that culminates in the hulking fat-rich bodies of seals, walruses, and whales. They range deep beneath the ocean, feeding on what people can't reach, and bringing sustenance close enough to harpoon.

Both history and future were visible even in the sand. Specifically, in a refrigerator-sized crater in the middle of the beach where sand ought to be. Ice lies under everything here. Until it doesn't. A melting ice lens beneath the beach left a yawning pit—as if a bomb had gone off, or more accurately, as though the beach had imploded—collapsing in on itself. Above the sand, chunks of peat crumbled from permafrost cliffs that line the shore, thawing into a shining wet mud. The Arctic was melting, eroding, hurrying toward a warmer and uncertain future.

In another few decades, Katmai-the-man could walk a brand-new coast of sand and bones and bear tracks here—more than a quarter mile inland—long after our current path recedes beneath the waves. In the rumpled expanse of the Chukchi, now a gray-blue infinity, he might pick out the towers of oil rigs or the blocky forms of ships bringing Arctic minerals to the cities of Asia. Along with the birds and wind, he might listen to the clattering passage of trucks full of coal.

◌◠◌

Only a few black pebbles were visible on the beach. Katmai recognized them by now, picking them out from the sea of gray stones with a cry of "Coal rock!" America's largest coal deposits are here, hidden beneath the tundra and extending for a thousand miles from where we stood. Few people know that most of the United States's coal lies beneath the Arctic. Even standing here, you might not know it. Back when commercial whaling ships plied these waters, Arctic coal fueled their burners, dug from small mines along the shore that have long since faded to invisibility. Since then, the coal has lain dormant, unmined and largely unexplored, far from industry, markets, and ports. There's oil here too, fifty or a hundred miles offshore in the Chukchi Sea, mirroring the oil deposits across Alaska's Arctic. Multinational oil coal companies have dipped their toes into Arctic exploration. They are fighting for the opportunity to drill on offshore leases. Shrinking sea ice makes drilling oil more feasible and shipping coal more attractive—as coal and oil burning shrinks the ice.

In the Arctic, nearly every convenience of modern life has to be shipped from far away. Fossil fuels power the planes that bring the soda and toys, the TVs that advertise them, the skiffs that hunt seals, the four-wheelers that carry berry-pickers, and the freezers that store raw caribou and salmon. An oil boom in the ocean or a coal boom on shore might bring a leap of new infrastructure and an economy of scale. It might halve the costs of chips and soda. It might halve the costs of skiff fuel and electric light. It might bring wealth to people here, or pass them right by. It might come to endanger the whales and caribou they still depend on—subsistence resources still abundant enough to remind us that once the whole world was as wild, remote, and rich in life.

Does cheaper fuel for a four-wheeler matter when the village has been washed away, and the caribou have migrated north, or vanished altogether? Maybe the oil here will never be drilled, and the coal never mined. But elsewhere it already has been. And the climate change caused by all that burning fuel is thawing the permafrost and melting the ice, transforming the Arctic just as quickly and irreversibly as anything else the modern world has brought here.

Some days we simply strolled on the beach. Watching Katmai's bare toes on sand, picking up pebbles, we might have been anywhere. Anywhere where a lone caribou might pass by, anywhere where we could spot two grizzly bears on a lunch break, and anywhere where the only people we saw in a week were a boatload of Native hunters in a skiff. Lagoons and ocean mirrored the sky. The Arctic was a brilliant, shining, see-everywhere world. But it was a rare day that let us shed our coats. Wind came often, and when it came, it howled along the beaches, gusting over the ridge tops with enough strength to snatch the breath out of our mouths.

I thought we had learned all the lessons of wind. We had slept—more than once—with wind that swirled snow to sting our faces and piled it to bury our tent. We had ridden packrafts over wind-whipped swells, and squinted against blowing sand, snow, hail, rain, and sleet. Wind had pummeled us and shrieked at us. It had followed us for months. We had followed it for longer—always enchanted by storm-shaped landscapes, always choosing to walk back into the wind.

Wind loomed large in all our daily planning. Hours before nightfall, we would peer at the map, analyzing slopes and valleys, guessing where both wind and bears might pass us by. The wind churned waves against the headlands, pelting our legs with sand. On the ridges, it tore at our faces, drowning out all other sounds until I could barely hear myself shouting "Old MacDonald" for Katmai—or Katmai shouting his own distress.

That night, we walked past hill after hill on a wind-blasted shore, seeking protection. My eyes followed the sweep of green and gold tundra up to lumps of rounded gray. The hills were too old, too smooth and round for the terrain to fold us into a windless pocket. Nothing was taller than a knee-high willow. Nothing but the cabin.

It was tilted so far off its foundation that walking inside was like scaling a steep hill. Who owned it? How recently had they been here? What had caused it to settle so dramatically sideways? I was always curious about wilderness cabins but usually avoided them. This one was our lucky break of the day. In Alaska, the spirit of hospitality extends beyond the presence of actual people, to unlocked cabins with unspoken invitations, asking for nothing more than respect. We propped up a plywood board for a level place to sleep, watching the waves froth from its sideways window.

The storm continued. Our luck ran out. The tent crumpled in and then sprung out again—its rhythm like a heavy breathing—in gusts that had only grown stronger. Wind tossed rain against our walls. The unpleasant prospect of leaving in the morning was quickly countered by the unpleasant prospect of staying in bed all day, doing nothing but increasing the chance that we would run out of food.

We ate on the beach, where a few pieces of driftwood washed far from their forest beginnings became a wind-whipped fire, dry kindling carefully carved from their hard white centers. Tongues of flame leaped sideways along the beach. Rain hit the hot rocks with a sizzling hiss, evaporating immediately. Those rocks were the only thing dry—unnaturally light against the now black beach. Hig squatted over the pot, steam billowing from his clothes. I crouched in an awkward hole in the rocks, peering at an ocean that was as forbidding as the sky. The rain came sideways, sneaking under the boulders to spatter on my hood. Hot soup and scalding coffee fought back against its chill.

I tied Katmai on me in a hurried fumble, my wet-cold fingers reluctantly pulled from the protection of sleeves. On top of it all, my raincoat was stretched to near-bursting to fit over both me and Katmai, the pouch of food I carried on my chest, and my ever-growing belly. Rain swept our backs, soaking through the worn-out fabric, seeping around Katmai's head through the slit I'd cut in the back, wetting both of us.

The world was too cold to play in for more than a few minutes at a time, and Katmai spent most of his day under my coat, spending our breaks snuggled up to nurse. He wasn't verbal enough yet to whine. It may have been a blessing. But it was also a worry. I kept a constant watch on his temperature, feeling his hands, reaching my own cold fingers under his coat to feel the warmth of his small chest. Katmai's younger sibling kicked away from within my womb, warming me with the fiery metabolism of pregnancy.

Blowing rain is some of the coldest weather. We walked through another day of blowing rain, slept through another night of blowing rain, and woke up the next morning to find the blowing rain sharing our tent with us.

"Maybe the wind is just blowing condensation from the inside wall, and that's what's spraying us," Hig suggested.

"No way, it's way too much water for that. It's definitely coming *through*," I insisted. "Did we seal the seams well enough?"

"Maybe not, but I doubt that's the problem. Remember, the last tent worked even without sealing it at all."

"And this is basically the same tent! Could it be different somehow, or is this just somehow a much worse place than we've *ever* set up in a storm?" I felt betrayed by the tent. I loved our tent. It was a twin of the shelter we'd carried for four thousand miles two years earlier, missing only the rents left by bear claws in our previous copy. But another overnight shift in wind, coupled with a total lack of anything to hide behind, had proved too much for the thin silnylon walls. I wondered if we'd had the same trouble before, and had simply glossed over it in our memories.

We left our wet sleeping bags to walk in wet clothes through a wet and fog-shrouded world. A trio of musk-ox silhouettes ambled by in the misty distance. We squatted briefly in a soggy meadow, picking a few ripe cloudberries as we waited for the water to boil on another sideways fire. The Arctic's short summer was already turning to fall. The mosquitoes were nearly gone, and reds and golds had begun to creep over the tundra. I'd remembered that fall storms could be exciting—that they could make a coastline come alive. This time, it just seemed wet.

A three-mile backtrack brought us to an unfinished and unheated cabin—this one square on its foundation—where the only amenities were a roof and four rainproof walls. Hig cooked our dwindling food on a fire outside, while Katmai vroomed a headlamp across the bare plywood with enthusiastic motor sounds. The eventual end of the storm would bring calmer water, which would let us paddle a small channel in a long spit—the last obstacle between us and the village of Point Hope. From Point Hope, we had three more weeks ahead of us. Wrapping myself in the sleeping bag, I dreamed about the villages I was eager to visit, the wildlife I was eager to encounter, and the hundreds of miles of terrain I was eager to see. Storms always end.

I listened to the spatter of inconvenient rain, waiting for its trickling chill to be swept away by the moments of glory.

7: Arctic Life

THE STORM'S SHADOW had lifted to reveal a stripe of sand with whale bones scattered to a distant horizon. Four-wheeler tracks drew their lines on that sand, between crumbling permafrost bluffs and the surf of the Chukchi Sea. At the top of the bluffs, bright red and orange cloudberries speckled the tundra. I bobbed up and down like a bird, shoes squelching in the muck, grabbing the berries as Katmai clamored for them. We were approaching the village of Point Hope in the northwest corner of Alaska, around two hundred miles north of the Arctic Circle.

Stooped figures in the distance, a handful of women stood next to their four-wheelers, filling plastic buckets with cloudberries. The raspberry's tundra cousin, each multilobed berry stands on its own three-inch-tall stalk, pointing at the sky from a blanket of sphagnum moss and swamp. Their slightly fermented sweetness melts in hand and mouth, or piles into delicious goo with the cookie fragments at the bottom of a ziplock bag. I fell a few paces behind Hig, suddenly shy as we approached the first of the strangers.

"You must be the folks from Seldovia!" the woman declared, standing up from where she was stooped among the berries. "I'm Aggie. I heard you

Evening light bathes a cabin on the coast south of Point Hope.

were coming." Her friends walked over to join our conversation, carrying their own buckets of berries. We knew no one in Point Hope. But a few days ago, a group of hunters had passed us in a skiff, sparking a few moments of shouted conversation. That was enough.

Learning that we'd never eaten muktuk (bowhead whale blubber), Aggie pulled out a container full of the rubbery black and white morsels, thrusting it toward us: "This is from the best part of the flipper." The muktuk was soon followed by smoked salmon, bottles of juice, salmon sandwiches, and a packet of fruit snacks. I chewed a piece of muktuk, gingerly at first, passing another piece over my shoulder to Katmai. It was better than I expected—reminiscent of coconut. As we chatted, I relaxed out of my shyness, once again appreciating the joy in the connection—the reason I look forward to every town as much as the wilderness between them.

Our adventures never collide with other adventurers, striding across the wilderness toward their own arbitrary goals. They certainly never collide with the tiny population of modern adventuring families. Alaska's too big for that. Yet here in the villages, journeys like ours are only a generation or two in the past, when people navigated without the help of maps, ate without the help of grocery stores, and carried no satellite-linked electronic panic buttons. When they walked with babies and kids and grandmothers and all of their worldly possessions. When they walked because they needed to get somewhere. Maybe all our planning and concern was an artifact of modernity. Even a hundred years ago our "expeditions"—lacking modern technology—would be vastly more difficult than they are today. And they would be simply a part of an ordinary life. No one walks now. Their goals are less arbitrary than ours—usually hunting or gathering—and much more efficiently met by the four-wheelers, skiffs, and snow machines that have made travel so much faster. But everybody has a story about their grandfather walking over the same hills we'd traveled.

The women cooed over Katmai. He stared at them warily from my back, fussing shyly if they got too close, eating the food they'd broken out especially for him, oscillating between fascination and exhaustion. When Hig and I decided to have a child, we knew that unlike our expeditions, this was a journey that billions had taken before us. A one-and-a-half-year-old is a universal; a natural conversation starter; a point of connection.

I first stepped into a Native village as a new college graduate, visiting Alaska for a summer of adventure. Now I was a pregnant mother of a toddler, visiting from another little village a few hundred miles to the south. We talked about kids. We talked about our own berry harvest back home. We were a family, traveling at a family's speed. As we move farther from the world of single-white-male adventurers, we find that people seem to see us differently. Before, we'd been just one more set of crazy young white kids collecting an experience of the "Last Frontier." As adventurers-with-kid, though, we were probably more unusual than we'd ever been. For adventurers.

But here, at Point Hope, we were only more normal. We were a family, who lived close to our own extended family. We were rural. Alaskan. Non-native, and brand-new to the Arctic, we were still nowhere close to local, but we'd moved much closer to their world.

⤨

Point Hope was first named Tikigaq—the index finger—for the long, narrow spit it sits on. With a lagoon behind and the Chukchi Sea before it, this low-lying spine of sand and tundra points straight into the ocean. Ancient house pits uncovered by archaeologists show us that people have lived here for at least twenty-six hundred years. The new town is only a few decades old, moved to escape the encroaching sea, backing up against the lagoon that lines the landward shore. Dense clumps of small wooden houses sit on a lifeless pad of gravel, a mile or two inland from the old sod huts. Laid out in a modern grid, four-wheeler shortcuts and footpaths are slowly giving the town a more organic shape. A modern sewer system hides beneath the gravel. Powerlines crisscross town, running freezers that are gradually replacing the last permafrost ice cellars. Warming soil renders them unreliable anyway.

This was the closest they could get to living in the sea. Cartoon drawings of bowhead whales decorate buildings, and jawbones decorate the graves of whalers past. Visiting with an elder, we sat on wooden chairs beside a small square table, in a wood-paneled room covered with family photographs. Elijah rummaged in his fridge, bringing out plates of muktuk and raw whale meat, explaining the best way to eat them while spinning stories of his childhood—as a nomadic reindeer herder in a sod hut. He watched Katmai devour thin rubbery slices of blubber, eyes lit up in his crinkled face at the sight of that enjoyment, describing his crusade to ensure that whaling could survive in Point Hope.

Five hundred years after the Point Hopers began to hunt Arctic bowheads, commercial whalers moved in on them. By 1914, the bowheads numbered fewer than a tenth of their former abundance, and the New England whalers, who had sailed thousands of miles to reach this sea from the picked-over whaling grounds of the Atlantic, disappeared with them. The Eskimos remained. In the 1970s, concerned about low population numbers, the International Whaling Commission sought to ban the subsistence harvest of bowheads in Alaska. The villagers responded with a commission of their own, forming the Alaska Eskimo Whaling Commission in 1977, made up of representatives from eleven Arctic villages.

"I talked in my Native language about whaling and what it means to me to all those senators," Elijah reminisced. "And they listened." Today, the Eskimo Whaling Commission manages the harvest in a joint program with NOAA (the National Oceanic and Atmospheric Administration). Between them, the villages take around forty whales a year, using a combination of modern technology and ancient skills.

"More mup-nup!" Katmai crowed.

Elijah turned to Katmai, smiling. "Your Eskimo name is Olugharock. And you have to come back here and be a whale hunter someday." I wrote the name down as best I could, but Elijah couldn't spell it for me. He had never learned the white man's way of writing his native language.

⌒⌒

The small store in Point Hope sells mainly candy and soda. At the school picnic we attended, people ate from paper plates piled with hot dogs and chips. But the school mascot is the Harpooners. We followed four-wheeler tracks out of town as we'd followed them in, on a smooth sand beach that felt almost hot in the rare sunny calm. After a couple hours' walk, we ran into a pair of children playing on the beach. A boy and a girl, maybe nine or ten years old, practiced their archery and threw harpoons at a pile of scrap wood. They invited us white folks to give it a try. I missed entirely. Hig did a little better. The kids did best.

"I'm going to kill a whale!" the boy proclaimed confidently.

"Me too!" the girl jumped in. "When I grow up, I'm going to be a hunter, and I'm going to hunt seals and whales and caribou and bears!"

"My uncle shot a bear right there," the boy gestured nearby, clearly proud.

It seemed at the same time endearingly cute and eerily bloodthirsty. And in the Arctic, practical. In the farm-unfriendly climate of the far north, people have always fed themselves on the animals and on the wealth of the sea.

We came to the Arctic thinking of coal, but the stories we heard were about whales and oil, and the uneasy tension between these two resources that propped up the world. The Arctic is built on rocks saturated with oil. From Prudhoe Bay, around 450 miles to the east, billions of barrels have been pulled from the ground. Oil runs the state government, provides dividends to residents, powers cars and four-wheelers and planes, warms houses, and builds schools and sewer systems in remote villages. And there is oil beneath the Chukchi Sea. Shell Oil paid $2.1 billion for a set of offshore oil leases here, setting off a series of challenges from local villages and environmental groups seeking to block the drilling. Shell eventually received approval, but the company's plans have been stymied by failures of critical equipment, failures to meet regulatory standards, and a drill rig run aground on an Alaska island. As of early 2013, they have yet to drill into the actual zone of oil.

Oil conjures visions of money, and visions of disaster—bringing up images of oil-slicked otters from the Exxon Valdez spill in Prince William Sound and oil-slicked pelicans from the more recent Deepwater Horizon spill in the Gulf of Mexico. In Point Hope, a gravel road leads to a protected beach, where the town's fleet of skiffs is pulled up on the sand. There are no other boats. If oil spilled here, what could anyone do about it? What would happen to the whales? Would oil development destroy the world as they know it? Or provide an economic boom? Or neither? Or both? The possibilities created an uneasy tension in this oil-dependent village, in an oil-dependent state, in an oil-dependent world.

"Look at all the heat in our houses here," Elijah had pointed out. "I don't think people will go back to seal oil and wood, or even coal."

An oil spill would be a disaster. And a successful drilling operation would be a disaster. Much of the pro-drilling rhetoric focuses on finding more oil—on the worry of running out, on the goal of having more, and the hope of making it more affordable to burn. But we already have more oil than we can afford to burn.

If Katmai were to come here as an adult—to walk the brand-new coastline after this one has disappeared beneath the sea—there will still be oil. Oil to fuel the plane that flies him here, and the planes that supply the village, and the four-wheelers they use for hunting. If the village is there at all. If the world continues on our current path, we will use up the entire global "carbon budget" by the time Katmai finishes high school. Going over that budget—putting any more fossil carbon in the atmosphere—pushes us beyond the reach of any climate that scientists have tagged as "safe." Even today, these Arctic villages aren't safe from the changes we've wrought. We can't afford to find more oil.

〰️

South of Point Hope village, we paddled around Cape Thompson. Birds floated at the invisible intersection between the calm gray ocean and the thick fog hovering above. As the clouds slowly rose from the glassy surface of the Chukchi, castle-like spires appeared before us, stretching into the sky. "Ee-owh-eee-owh-ee-owh," Katmai called excitedly from my back, imitating the raucous screeching of the murres and kittiwakes that speckled the cliffs and wheeled in circles above us.

In between the whalers and the oil men, it was the nuclear scientists who set their sights on this piece of the world. Not for the resources it contained, but for what it *didn't* have—visibility and political clout. In the 1950s, a river valley south of the village was chosen by the Atomic Energy Commission to be the site of Project Chariot. Nuclear bombs to equal the blast of 160 Hiroshimas were to be detonated beneath the tundra to create a harbor no one needed, in a place so remote they thought no one would object, to provide a shining example of the peaceful use of nuclear weapons. The villagers of Point Hope reached out to the world to stop the plan, joined by scientists working on preliminary studies, and eventually the larger environmental movement. In 1962, the idea was abandoned.

Today, the Ogotoruk Valley looks like every other wild swath of berry bushes and scrubby willow. The buildings used by nuclear scientists and engineers are gone. The contaminated soil from radioactivity experiments has been removed. Only a shack on the tundra marks what once was, and what might have been. This coast escaped the nuclear bombs. It may escape an oil spill, and coal strip mines. Local villagers have a strong history of opposing the changes that threaten them. But the biggest threat of all is one that most people spoke of as a foregone conclusion. The climate change that is destroying their world seems so far beyond the power of a few small towns. What can they do about the warming?

Seventy-five miles of coastline later, we approached the next village, Kivalina, on another spit of sand. On this coast, we walked a series of long and skinny islands, where one beach faced the sea and one faced an inland lagoon. We rafted across the lagoon mouth openings to hop between them. A mile inland, low hills rose abruptly from the flat plain behind the lagoons. Their edge was once a beach as well, dozens of feet higher than the current one. That farther shore dates from the age *before* the last ice age. It's a clue from the last time the planet was warm.

On average, the world then was about two degrees Celsius (3.6 degrees Fahrenheit) warmer than today. That's the same two degrees that has often been set as a "target" that might help us avoid the most catastrophic impacts of climate change. The same two degrees that models now predict will be pretty catastrophic after all. The same two degrees used to set that global "carbon budget"—the one we're on track to exceed by the time Katmai is an adult.

On average, the sea level before the last ice age was more than twenty feet higher than today. What does that mean for the sand spits that house the modern villages? The tundra flats of berries that stretch back to the distant hills? All the oil and coal that humans have burned over the past century has already added 0.8 degrees Celsius to global temperatures. By the end of this next century, the whole world will probably reach the temperature it held when that distant shoreline was cut. Sea level will follow. Not quickly, but inevitably.

Climate change is happening to all of us, in a pile of droughts and storms that come with ever greater frequency, dwarfing the weather of our childhoods. Most of the time, we can still ignore climate change—its importance wavering with politics and election cycles and whatever the weather was last week. But the Arctic warms more and faster than the rest of the world. Here, the warming is everyone's worry—an escalating crisis they've been dealing with for decades, a rising flood threatening to sweep away their villages as it transforms their lives.

"The tundra used to reach way out to there," the Kivalina elder gestured out to sea, "until the global warming came." His name was Joe, and he showed us the decaying whalebone frames and the outlines of house pits of the old Kivalina. He talked about the thin ice that now made hunting dangerous, the erosion that was eating away at the town, and their efforts to find a place to move. In population, Kivalina is about the same size as Seldovia—around four hundred people. But in physical space, it's much smaller—perched on a narrow spit between the Chukchi Sea and the lagoon behind, with the Wulik River channel right at the edge of town. Water surrounds it on three sides, and erosion has pushed Kivalina to the very edge of their runway on the fourth side. A seawall of light gray boulders shipped 350 miles from Nome tries to hold the ocean at bay.

Kivalina is crowded, vulnerable, and precarious. Where it sits, it's not long for this world. As the permafrost thaws, the coastline crumbles. Thawing and crumbling riverbanks muddy the town's water supply, and colonizing beavers have brought giardia parasites to a region that never hosted them before. The ice that shields the coast from waves is thinner and slower to form each year. Before the seawall, houses fell into the sea. Not a single structure in town is above the reach of a storm.

The villagers have been debating for years about where to move the town. Across the river (on another sand spit) would give them a place similar to where they live now, but not currently subject to rapid erosion. No one can tell them how long that spot might be safe. If sea level rise accelerates as expected, the relocated town might not last much longer than the old one. At a spot farther inland, they would gain more distance from the encroaching water but lose their close connection to the ocean for fishing and hunting—the backbone of the culture. Neither location would take them above the ancient shoreline at the base of the hills, but it will probably be centuries before the sea rises that far. Of over two hundred Native villages in Alaska, most face risks from flooding and erosion. Thirty-one face imminent threats. Four, including Kivalina, are in need of a wholesale relocation—sooner rather than later.

In Kivalina, modern-looking faucets sit unused and unfunctional. Water rests in clean rubber garbage cans, filled and hauled from the town's central tank. Curtains screen off closetlike bathrooms, where reeking honey buckets are lined with white plastic trash bags. In permafrost, there can be no outhouses. So those white plastic bags are tied off, and towed by four-wheeler to the dump a mile and a half away. Sometimes that dump floods too, mixing that sewage with the waters of the lagoon. A village in limbo, Kivalina is one of the few Alaskan communities still lacking any form of water or sewer system. No one will invest in infrastructure for a temporary community.

Each time Hig and I stepped onto the streets of Kivalina, an entourage of children engulfed us. Despite being barely larger than Seldovia in population, this town seemed to have at least ten times the number of children, freely roaming in packs at all hours of the day.

"What color is your hair, Katmai?"

"Whiiite!"

"What color are your shoes, Katmai?"

"Bwack!" he crowed happily.

Katmai had these answers down pat. They'd asked him the same thing five minutes ago. They'd asked him the same questions yesterday, when we spent the day hopping classrooms at the school, showing pictures and talking with the kids. Somehow, the children never seemed to tire of hearing his high-pitched squeak of response. With his glowing white-blond hair and charming toddler voice, Katmai stood out even more than we did. Some of the kids tried to pick him up, while others held his hands, and still others passed him rocks to throw. They pointed out toys for him to play with. He pointed out every piece of trash. They asked me who taught him to talk. They asked me how old he was. They marveled at the colorful wrap I used to carry him, waving it like a banner. I marveled at the seemingly effortless way babies here were carried in their parent's or sibling's coats—no extra device required.

⌒⌒

Our base camp in Kivalina was a sleeping bag on a mattress, in an empty bedroom of a new-looking house, large compared to most of the houses in town. Miles before we reached Kivalina, we'd run into Della, the woman who owned the house, as she headed out of town on her four-wheeler. She had offered us a place to stay for a few days. Supposedly she lived here with her children, but residences were fluid, and often there was no one there but us.

"I don't like how empty it is here," Della admitted, sitting on a couch in the large, bare living room. "I spend most of my time at my sister's." There, a crowd of people filled a much smaller space. One-year-old twins sucked on popsicles, adults chatted, and older children rotated in and out from playing outside. Some of the children lived in Della's sister's house. Some were siblings of the children who lived there but had been adopted by the grandparents a few houses away. Some were cousins, others were friends. I lost track after the first two introductions and stopped trying to puzzle out the relationships. Everyone seemed to be some sort of family.

In the Arctic's summer light, nothing happens early, and we chatted for hours as dinner was being assembled, snacking on a bowl of fresh cloudberries and pilot bread crackers, drinking Coke.

"Knife or ulu?" Della's brother-in-law asked us, gesturing to a pair of chairs at the table. The village had just caught a beluga whale a few days earlier, and a bowl of boiled beluga blubber was the centerpiece of the meal. Surrounding it were dishes full of raw dried caribou, raw frozen bowhead blubber, and raw frozen fish. Each diner piled a paper plate with their favorites, cutting small slices with a knife or ulu, occasionally adding a shake of salt or a squirt of yellow mustard to the meat before picking it up with greasy fingers.

The boiled beluga blubber was surprisingly delicious. Katmai agreed, and my knife was kept busy for the first half of the meal just cutting pieces for him. Our hosts smiled at the sight of the tiny white boy so enthusiastic about Native foods, and gave him another Eskimo name—this one meaning "sun." The one-year-old twins watched from the carpet, soaking in their world. Maybe they will grow up to carry babies under their coats, harpoon whales, and fix meals of beluga and caribou. Maybe an older Katmai will return to the Arctic and join them in their feast. I hoped that if they wanted to, they'd have the chance. But none of them will do it here. "Here" will be gone already.

8: Running with Red Dog

AUGUST HAD TURNED to September. In the hills of the Arctic, fall was already well under way. As we ducked through the patches of willows that lined each creek, yellow-green leaves rained down on Katmai's head, each step a colorful shower. "More through bush!" he yelled with delight.

The whole rainbow was represented: in scarlet bearberries, orange dwarf birch, sun-yellow cottonwood, yellow-green willows, lime-green alders, and the purple-pink blueberry bushes with their weight of indigo fruit. Hig's turquoise jacket stood out brilliantly. My yellow jacket blended right in. But as the tundra plants painted the ground in kaleidoscopic glory, the sky weighed us down with its ominous gray, spitting out a never-ending series of rain squalls. The rain seeped into our shoes and socks from the soggy ground, flapped at our torn rainpants from the drops on the bushes, blew sideways into our hoods, and drizzled down from above. The bright leaves glowed even brighter against the glowering sky.

Fall is the season of the windstorms that had battered us on Cape Lisburne and had sent us scuttling for the shelter of a cabin on the way to Point Hope. Fall is the season of a damp chill that seems like it will never let me go. It's the season of rain that lasts for days, blotting out the mountains in a wash of gray.

Autumn scatters leaves in a tributary of the Noatak River.

I expected all of this. In our dreams, fall storms had become a positive—something exciting and adventurous. With climate change shrinking
the beaches, storms were some of the most dramatic and immediate challenges that faced this coast. I knew that nonstop rain squalls came wrapped
and tied with a ribbon of fall colors and an abundance of berries. Who
wouldn't choose a little rain and cold over the early summer's hordes of
mosquitoes? These were good, solid reasons to embrace the season. They
relied, as always, on the human brain's failure to remember the visceral truth
of wet and cold. But they weren't all of the reasons, or maybe even the most
important. We traveled during fall so we could have our cake and eat it too,
pushing this trip as late as we dared to preserve every possible moment of
summer at home in Seldovia. To preserve it literally: filling freezers and jars
with blueberries and salmonberries, beets and broccoli, carrots and kale and
bright red salmon fillets.

We could afford to feed ourselves through a winter without these
frozen treasures. And unlike people in these Arctic villages, I had no long
tradition of subsistence to maintain. I was a new gardener, a new fisherman, a new Alaskan. But even for the sake of a drier adventure, I wasn't
quite willing to give up that newfound connection to my own patch of
ground. I had spent the summer wishing I had more time at home. Now, as
the sky drenched us yet again, I was spending some of the fall wondering if
I ought to have traded a few gallons of berries for the chance to walk here
before the rain.

⌒⌒

It rained all night. For the last two days we'd been circling around a low
ridge of shattered rock, our hopes perking with each lull. We could climb
it in the rain, but what we wanted was the view. I wasn't very hopeful
anymore. But when we finally dragged ourselves out of the tent, the sky had
risen and lightened to a drier, smoky hue.

Our gray and yellow tent nearly disappeared below us as we climbed,
blending into the fall-colored willow bushes and slopes of rock. I imagined
soldiers trying to camouflage themselves here, forced to dress in pink and
yellow in this gaudy world. To the south, the Noatak River appeared as a

shining distant curve. Northeast, we could see what we'd been looking for: Red Dog Mine.

Red Dog was different. It wasn't about coal or oil or climate change or a prospect floating in an uncertain future. Red Dog was about zinc and lead, and solidly real. The mine pit itself was hidden behind a mountain, but through the shifting base of the cloud we now sat in, we could see brightly painted buildings, the end of the tailings pond, and the long stripe of the runway. I pointed it out to Katmai over my shoulder. "Look. There's Red Dog Mine."

"Red Dog Mine nice?" he piped back.

"I don't know," I told him. "That's not an easy question." In Katmai's world, every object we encountered was either "nice" or "bad." I had no qualms emphasizing the "badness" of unknown mushrooms and poisonous plants, but even telling him the beach trash was "bad" made me a little uneasy—uncomfortable with my role in promoting a black-and-white categorization of the world. This glimpse through the fog was our last view of a mine we'd been orbiting for over a week. That week had only made me less sure of my answer.

Four days earlier, Red Dog had first appeared as barns fit to house a herd of mastodons. Constructed in a flag-inspired pattern of red, white, and blue, the ore-storage barns at Red Dog Port are the largest buildings in the state—more than twenty million cubic feet for the larger one alone. These are the solution to Arctic winters, storing ore through all the months of sub-zero snow, awaiting the brief ice-free shipping season.

Along with the ore barns, an array of barracks and other facilities squatted on the tundra south of Kivalina in hulking rectangles, ending in a dock protruding into the Chukchi Sea. A giant ship waited offshore in deeper water, loaded by an alternating series of ore-filled barges. From there, Red Dog reaches inland along a fifty-two-mile road, to another great grouping of colorful buildings, an endless parade of enormous yellow trucks, and the black maw of the mine pit itself. Red Dog is the second-largest producer of zinc in the world, and the richest mine in Alaska. It's the biggest thing in the Northwest Arctic and could easily swallow every neighboring village.

Red Dog is *inside* every village too. Before we could see the mine itself, we were inundated by the iconic symbol of a happy red dog and the words "Red Dog Mine," which graced tote bags and sweatshirts throughout the village of Kivalina. Over half of Red Dog's 475 workers are Northwest Arctic Native Association (NANA) shareholders—Native Alaskan residents and stakeholders in the regional Native corporation that is half owner of the mine.

"Back when they were deciding whether to do the mine," said one Red Dog worker, "the thing that finally convinced the elders was that young people could stay in the villages. Back when I was a kid, everyone had to leave for boarding school in high school, and there were only a few of the men in town that had jobs. More than the money even, they wanted the jobs, so all the young people didn't have to leave." Hundreds of jobs, appearing where none were before. Red Dog manages to be a significantly local operation, bringing home money and benefits that are promised by all industrial projects but less often delivered. The mine is the only taxpayer in its entire borough and pays hundreds of millions in taxes and royalties each year. Money flows to the borough, the state, the nation, and to dozens of struggling communities. Through a revenue-sharing provision created when the Native corporations were formed, Red Dog Mine contributes money to village and regional Native corporations across the state—even those a thousand miles away.

ᗯᗡᗯ

Approaching the Red Dog dock, we left our footprints on top of the ubiquitous four-wheeler tracks, nervously nearing the buildings we'd been watching for days. The port facilities loomed to our left, a few vehicles slowly moving between them. My curiosity was tempered by the clear warning signs. Beach walking—fine. Going anywhere else—not allowed.

I had resigned myself to giving Red Dog a wide berth. It actually seemed like a bit of a relief. Simpler. Then a truck zoomed down to the dock. The young Native man inside it shrugged at the bizarre appearance of a white family on foot and our requests for a tour. He made a quick radio call on our behalf, and soon we were swept up in the warm embrace of the mine PR force. They dropped us in the manager's lap, across a shining round table in a mostly empty cafeteria of linoleum and yogurt cups, answering all our questions with a string of impressively large numbers: fourteen million gallons of fuel burned a year, two hundred metric tons of ore on a truck, half a million tons of ore on a barge, nine hundred million tons of ore in a year. I scribbled each figure down dutifully, failing to conceptualize any of them.

We slept in Red Dog beds, scrubbed in Red Dog showers, ate a Red Dog breakfast, then buckled into a Red Dog van with Jim, a mine PR representative, for the fifty-two-mile drive to the mine itself. There are trips where we refuse all motorized rides. We had made no firm rules for this Arctic journey, but a fifty-two-mile hitch gave me pause. A fifty-two-mile walk on a dusty road full of giant ore trucks did as well. Jim tipped the balance in the end: *Take the ride, and I'll give you a tour of the mine.* The van zipped along the smooth gravel, keeping in constant radio chatter with the trucks that occasionally hurtled past us. Jim's a PR guy. Swooping visitors into a bubble of reassuring answers is part of his job. So is meeting with villagers.

While the village of Noatak is closest to the mine, Kivalina lies downstream. Discharges from the mine end up in the Wulik River and eventually in Kivalina's drinking water. Residents have sued Red Dog over violations of their discharge permits, setting off a multiyear legal battle. In Kivalina, we asked one man we met what he thought of Red Dog as a neighbor. He paused for a minute, then answered cautiously: "Except for all the pollution, they're a good neighbor." He explained that when the mine got started, it caused a big fish kill in the river, and even now villagers could taste the difference in the water.

As soon as we brought up Kivalina, Jim sighed. "We got off on the wrong foot with that town," he explained—confirming the fish kill but emphasizing that all those problems had been cleared up long ago. "Back in the 1980s when this mine got started," he said, "no one thought about those things." Things like lead and zinc dust blowing off the trucks and on the road. Like the risks to humans and fish from total dissolved solids in the water. From Jim's point of view, the villagers were stubbornly refusing to accept the scientific evidence that Red Dog's current practices posed no danger to their water or the wildlife they depend on. He thought maybe some of the villagers were suing in the hopes they might get money to relocate their village—in essence, pinning Red Dog with the impacts of climate change—not because they saw actual problems with the mine.

In 2008, Kivalina also sued Exxon Mobil—pinning them quite directly with the impacts and costs of climate change. The case was dismissed, on the grounds that solving climate change lies in the hands of politicians.

Through a screen of gray drizzle, the Red Dog site looked apocalyptic. Big yellow trucks crawled along winding paths, piled with black ore, dwarfed by the maw of the black pit they traveled in. The orange stain of oxidized metals ran bright stripes down dark pit walls. Muddy rivulets of water stained a similar orange flowed into culverts, headed toward the water treatment plant. Jim forbid me to take photographs.

Despite the mine's 475 workers, barely a human was anywhere to be seen—all were hidden within the confines of trucks and buildings. Beside the pit, waste rock was heaped in great piles. All of this rock, and its ground-up remains in the tailings pond, is classified as toxic waste by the Environmental Protection Agency (EPA). Its sheer volume brings Red Dog to the top of the list in the nation's annual "Toxics Release Inventory."

It's just rock. But it's rock that reacts with air and water to leach out acid. It's rock shattered by dynamite then pulverized into flour, millions of times faster than it could have eroded naturally. Jim spent a lot of time showing me around the various parts of the water treatment system. The dam to hold tailings and the lined sump to capture anything that makes it through the dam. The series of diversion trenches and pipes that keep clean water out of the mine and send contaminated water to the treatment plant. The giant settling tank where the metals precipitate after lime is added and the culvert that spits water into Red Dog Creek at the end of it all, where Jim took a drink straight from the pipe. A classic mine PR move. It is impressive—all the careful thought and calculation that goes into water management. It's also impressively complicated.

Red Dog's closure plan states that when the mine eventually closes, they'll still need seven year-round workers—fifteen in the summer—to run a plant treating 1.4 billion gallons of water each year for, in the words of one manager, "as long as it snows and rains here." To do that, they'll keep their port open, shipping in seventy-three hundred tons of lime annually, mixing it with toxic acid water to settle heavy metals into seventy thousand tons of sludge. That sludge will be funneled into ponds, frozen in sheets in the winter and then stored somewhere, filling the mine pit until eventually it overwhelms the space—within a hundred years—and a new spot must be found. This will cost ten million dollars each year. To pay for it all, an investment made today must generate ten million in interest every year . . . forever.

Someone at Red Dog has researched all of those numbers, typing them into a plan of optimistic impossibility. But that future was beyond the bounds of Jim's well-practiced answers. He acknowledged the inevitable then pushed it aside. "Maybe, eventually, there's a point where we just don't care anymore. Maybe society has other issues by then." Red Dog's problem is the problem of nearly every modern metal mine. We'd heard a similar story a few years earlier, as a state employee described the potential "forever" of the proposed Pebble Mine, near Bristol Bay. For that maybe-mine—still only an idea—there were fewer numbers, a vaguer story, and much greater salmon rivers downstream. But the basic problem remains the same: tailings never disappear. It's no different across all the Superfund sites and acidic rivers that speckle the American West—legacies of mining past. We haven't solved this problem yet.

But perhaps society *will* have other issues by then. Perhaps society will have mine water-treatment plants scattered in every river valley, bonds that don't come close to paying for them all, climate-change increased storms that overwhelm them, and a world so awash in other hand-built problems that we can't afford to care. Perhaps it will be an easy choice, to abandon the Wulik River to remote and polluted obscurity.

Beyond the ridges that circle Red Dog, creeks wind south, through tundra that gives way to scrubby willows, disappearing beneath the northernmost fingers of cottonwood and spruce, then joining the wide swath of the Noatak River. We blew up our packraft on the muddy beach of a small back channel, between the carcasses of salmon, the prints of grizzly bears, and a set of boot tracks—the first human sign since we'd left the mine four days earlier. We floated past a group of three men fishing. A skiff zoomed up the main channel, the family inside pausing to chat with us before heading upstream. Trees hung over eroding banks at every turn.

"Uh-oh trees! Fall Noh-tak! Splash!"

We followed the current's braided path to the village of Noatak, as the sky returned to storm. It was another day's paddle to the gleaming promise of an invitation offered by that family in the skiff—to turn their mudroom into a jumble of clothes and gear and grit and stored-up rain. No matter how many times I experience it, the feeling of a hot shower followed by dry clothes on a cold, wet body is nothing but bliss. And the warmth of hospitality is always a beautiful surprise.

Noatak was the last village on our route. Talking to Robert, our host, we discovered he was a good friend of a Seldovia family we knew. He was a minister turned Red Dog human resources worker, adoptive father of several, who'd felt called by God to work at the mine. He felt like he could reach out to the young people working at the mine through HR, continuing his own form of ministerial work. Robert saw Red Dog as a force of good in his world—providing jobs and reducing the astronomical costs of things shipped in, from gas to building materials.

We left the village for a slow and lazy float down the Noatak River, interspersed with shortcuts over golden tundra ridges, photographing nonchalant muskox. Toward the end of a trip, our minds begin to wander, the future overtaking the present in our conversations. We hashed out plans for the next expedition—exactly one year out—where we planned to live for months on the Malaspina Glacier with Katmai and the little one we still hadn't met.

"Do we really want to do the next big trip in the fall again?" I asked.

"Sure. I think our plan is pretty good. What's the problem?"

"Nothing really. This trip has been awesome, but it has been so wet, and I wonder if we're really making the best trade-offs by pushing the edges of the season."

"Those fall high-tide storms have the potential to bring some of the most interesting changes on that coast. That's what we're going to see. And the light," Hig reminded me. "Remember how amazing that coast was in the fall? The sunrises and sunsets over the waves. . . . Besides, it's never *always* raining."

"True." It wasn't raining now, and the setting sun stretched our shadows over the hill of flame-orange dwarf birch we were climbing. The little one we hadn't met was weighing me down more with every passing day, making me pant with exertion. I hoped he or she would be easier to carry on the outside.

We daydreamed farther into the future: was skiing on the Bering Sea coast doable with a two- and a four-year-old?

∞

We'd begun our voyage on a small plane chartered from the regional hub of Kotzebue. Three hundred miles later, we were returning there on our own power. The distance between us and the orange lights of Kotzebue had shrunk to two and a half miles of choppy brown. That few miles of open water was the longest crossing we'd ever done with three people piled into one small raft—probably the biggest obstacle of the entire journey. We debated sticking our thumbs out at one of the many skiffs cruising down the river back to town. But driven by both stubbornness and shyness, I never gave more than a friendly wave.

On the ocean's edge, the bushes had disappeared into grass and mudflats, pockmarked with the cracked dry outlines of caribou tracks. We boiled our final dinner at a driftwood duck blind, holding out threads and feathers to measure the strength and direction of the wind. A dozen white swans dotted the water in an arcing line. Our plan was on the edge. But maybe the conditions were good enough? The wind had been blowing for days—not very strong but steady, crosswise to our path. We peered into the distance, trying to estimate the waves. We could always turn around.

It was shallower than it looked. Hig began to walk straight out into the ocean's murky brown, wading past the flock of swans that erupted around us, pulling Katmai and me in the raft through the ankle-deep water on the edges of the sound. At knee-deep, he got in the raft, beginning to paddle. The bottom dropped away beneath the reach of the paddle blades. The waves grew, but never more than enough to slop occasional bits of water into the boat. Easy. An orange-pink sun dipped into the Chukchi Sea, while curious seals popped up all around us.

Paddling into Kotzebue the next morning, we looked up from our waterline perch at the tops of several-story buildings, towering over the flat land of sand and water surrounding them. Their bases were obscured by the tips of the small waves thumping the floor of our packraft. None of those front doors were more than a few feet above sea level. Kotzebue isn't eroding as quickly as Kivalina. It fights the ocean with seawalls. But as the water rises, and the storms grow, that strategy seems doomed to eventual failure.

In Kivalina, we had met a twelve-year-old boy who talked about his ambition to operate machinery at Red Dog when he grew up—a job that would let him continue to live in the village between his shifts at the mine. But Red Dog projects that it will run out of ore to mine in 2031. He'll be barely in his thirties. And Kivalina as we know it will be gone. Perhaps this young man will live in a brand-new inland community, one of the seven perpetual workers at the water treatment plant, protecting the land from the abandoned ghost of a mine.

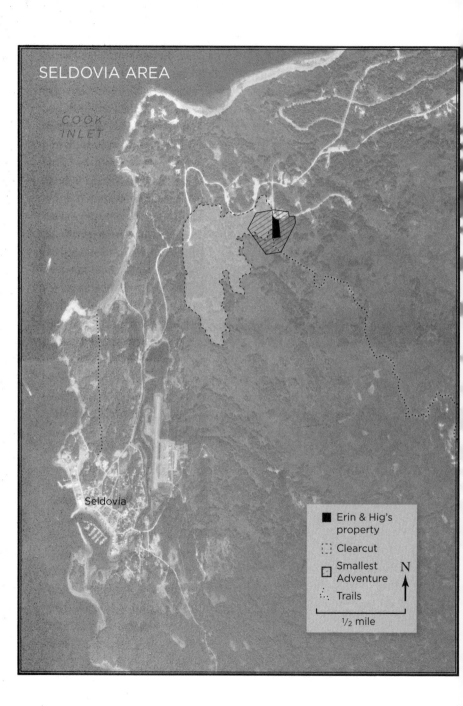

SELDOVIA AREA

COOK
INLET

Seldovia

■ Erin & Hig's
property

◌◌◌ Clearcut

▢ Smallest
Adventure

N

⋰ Trails

1/2 mile

PART III

The Village

9: An Inconvenient Paradise

IN THE HOMER FERRY office, I lifted a tiny sleeping lump out of a car seat and folded her into the long piece of fabric wrapped around my torso, feeling awkward and rusty at the task. I rocked on my feet, trying to soothe her back to sleep. Then I grabbed another wrap from our pile of coats and bags that was spilling over the floor—swinging it down to capture Katmai, where he wriggled on the slippery plastic seat. The end of the long piece of fabric swept my ticket onto the carpet. I squatted down, not entirely comfortably, picked up the ticket and scooped the almost-two-year-old onto my back. Wearing two children at once was something I had been thinking about ever since I'd discovered I was pregnant with my second. But the reality of it seemed sudden. Awkward. Heavy.

The sleet of the previous day had ended, leaving a network of slippery roads under a pale gray sky. Ice cleats on my feet, two kids strapped to my body, and one shopping bag in each hand, I strode toward the ferry as quickly as I was able to. My daughter had been born less than twenty-four hours ago. We were heading home.

With Lituya. My New Year's baby. My little girl.

Lituya the bay was five hundred miles away in Southeast Alaska, where

A local band brightens the winter with a concert in Seldovia's community center.

it provides the only harbor in 150 miles of storm-tossed sand. Dangerous rip currents guard the entrance to a pool of turquoise calm. The tongues of glaciers lap at its edges, where snowcapped peaks reach through ice sheets to the sky. For thousands of years, Lituya was a site of ancient villages. In 1958, it was the site of a seventeen-hundred-foot-high tsunami. The coast it is cut from—the Lost Coast—is one of the wildest and most remote parts of the state. It's one of my favorite places on earth.

Lituya the person was a squishy ten-pound lump against my chest, snuffling gently in her sleep as I sank into the ferry's padded seat. In the summer, this boat would be full of tourists. In the winter, the schedule shrinks from three trips a week to one, and nearly everyone on it is a Seldovian. We shared it today with a half-dozen others—good friends and casual acquaintances who had carried all our boxes and bags onto the boat— all helping us get home. Mountains rose up ahead of us—steep, craggy, and brushed with snow but only a few thousand feet high. Beneath them, a glimpse of our own brown roof, silvery smokestack, and its backdrop of dark trees and pillowy snow. Our familiar mountains, our snowshoe trail, our disorganized one-room life. My homesickness slowly collapsed into exhausted relief.

◡╱◠

Leaving Seldovia, or returning, is never simple. Not even in the fifteen miles that separates us from Homer. Homer is still over two hundred miles from the Anchorage airport. Anchorage is a three-and-a-half-hour flight from Seattle. Five and a half hours from Minneapolis. Nine and a half from New York. Putting all those steps together, it often takes days to leave the state— the strain of that distance taking a toll on anyone with family and friends far away.

The long series of connections that had been an exotic part of Sarah's *New York Times* adventure, which she'd reported on just over a year ago, was something else for the rest of us. Something I grumble about, and am grateful for. It's an isolation that turns a trip to the dentist or the building supply store into a major logistical operation. It's an isolation that keeps Seldovia small and close-knit—and our wilderness wild. In the warm bubble of a supportive community, surrounded by wild mountains and ocean, my life was absolutely simpler, cheaper, and freer than it had ever been before. But scanty job choices, five-dollar cartons of eggs, and a widening gulf between us and the rest of the country are the flip side of freedom.

~

A couple weeks later, I swung Katmai down from my back in a motion much smoother with practice. I shook snow off my coat, the wrap, his snowsuit and hat, trying to contain the chaos of gear that accompanies small people in the winter. On my chest, Lituya stayed asleep. Several three- to five-year-olds ran laps around the perimeter of the small house, shaking it with thundering footsteps. Katmai beelined for a pile of assorted toy vehicles, carefully vrooming them back and forth, then lining them up in neat rows on the couch cushions. Nearby, another almost-two-year-old did the same thing, and they gave each other sidelong glances as they played. I left Katmai to the toys and wandered into the kitchen, where a group of moms chatted while they set the table for lunch.

We began with the universal: the milestones, cute sayings, and particular quirks of each of our children; the dishes we'd brought to share; the recent weather. Then the conversations circled to the Seldovia particular: Did the snow stop long enough for the mail to come today? Is it cheaper to make a big trip across the bay to stock up on food, or pay for it to be shipped? What boots work best for winter tide-pooling?

This was a regular weekly gathering—all moms. Not by exclusion, but because all the dads worked, in traditional go-somewhere-every-day-and-get-paid-for-it jobs. Hig and I were different. We juggled. We traded roles in a complicated orbit between computer work, chores, and child care, using a system that has varied all the way from a detailed weekly schedule of two-hour time blocks to totally free-form: "Why don't you take the kids this morning and maybe I'll take them this afternoon?" Part-time consulting pays our small bills. Writing (for me) and running a nonprofit (for both of us) feeds our desire to do something in the world. Gardening and gathering is a decent help in feeding our family. Our jobs were in the yurt, but in an important way, they weren't in Seldovia at all—tied instead to a networked globe. It's a plan that means our income can fluctuate wildly. But in that flexibility I suspected I had an easier setup than anyone else in that gathering. I even had the helping hand of Katmai and Lituya's beloved Grandma Dede—close enough that our two-year-old could make the walk himself.

I counted children, ringing the table with mismatched chairs and stools, tiny plates, and little glasses. The food we were eating—all of it that didn't come from our own gardens and bays—was expensive. But the parenting wasn't. The only version of daycare in town is free, sponsored by the Seldovia Village Tribe. Nearly all the kids' activities are as well. There are always people to swap kids with, to chat with in the grocery store, to join up with on impromptu beach outings and hikes—or simply to stop by the house. We are all rich in neighbors.

At my neighbor Marcella's doorstep, a quarter mile from the yurt, I kicked the waffle-patterned wafers of snow from my boot treads, adding them to the slick-wet pile of footwear in the crowded entryway. A group of middle-aged women was gathered around the table, reminiscing about what the town had been like twenty years ago—when Hig was a student—as they gossiped about the school's latest hire.

"He's going to be a special ed aide."

"They're real outdoorsy people, and love to ski."

"We should hook them up to go skiing with Chris and Steve."

"I wonder if they're planning to have any kids?"

"The school is so much smaller than when I first moved here," Marcella commented, a little wistfully. She'd sent four kids through the Seldovia school—the oldest long grown and the youngest still in junior high.

Lituya was sleeping on my lap. Katmai was with Hig now but had been hanging on my leg for most of the morning. Between my own kids and our friends', I felt surrounded by children, but the Seldovia school hosts somewhere around fifty, half as many as it held when Hig was young. The town has maybe a couple dozen more besides, counting babies and toddlers and children who are homeschooled.

I listened quietly, getting a glimpse of the town's past and future that is harder to see through the lens of my handful of years here. The women talked about each year's shrinking school staff, tightening budgets, and collapsed classes that can span five years in age, where kindergarteners rub shoulders with fourth-graders. They talked about the loss of stores and year-round residents, and the proliferation of summer homes. Everyone has heard the saying *it takes a village to raise a child*. But living in an actual village, I was seeing the other side of that equation: *It takes children to keep a village alive.*

Hig and I adore our children, but even people I barely know seem to care about them more than I ever imagined. In a world where most places are overflowing with people, Seldovia is shrinking. Each of my pregnancies generated an almost palpable excitement—at neighborhood parties, in the grocery store and swimming pool, in people whose names I struggled to remember. Each child brings a little breath of life into the community, increasing the chances that other families will come or that existing ones will stay. And it's not just kids. Small numbers make every one of us important.

A few Seldovians are born each year. Usually a few die. One neighbor was buried in an avalanche near Anchorage. Another neighbor succumbed to a sudden and unexpected heart attack in the town weight room, in front of two of his children. That was Lowell, Marcella's husband—the hands behind the cozy house I was sitting in. Lowell had died only days ago, and this small gathering was one of the many expressions of community that had sprung up around that tragedy.

I didn't know Lowell all that well, but I knew his family. We'd made the quarter-mile walk to their house countless times, visiting Marcella, helping his daughter with her college application essay, eating homemade biscotti and salmon they'd caught and smoked themselves, joining in for potlucks and game nights. When Lituya was newly born, when Lowell was still alive, Marcella had stopped by with lingonberry jam and some of that smoked salmon in honor of our new-again parenthood. Now, I struggled to figure out what help we could possibly provide.

"Black chainsaw has a cord, so it's pretty quiet. Orange saw has an engine and it's pretty noisy," Katmai proudly pointed out, as he reached to touch the chainsaw riding next to him in the utility sled. The sled crunched heavily over packed-down snow as Hig dragged it up the road behind him.

A winter's weather writes a pattern on the land, each year's particular sequence of snows and melts laying on the ground like a fingerprint. There are drift times and ice times, hoarfrost and blizzards, and stretches of midwinter mud. This was the winter of the broken trees. Back in November, a freakish snowfall had weighted down the spruce trees with so much snow that many of them had snapped in half at the first slight breeze. We'd lost power for days. Now it was late January—nearly a month since Lituya's birth and around a week since Lowell's death. Throughout our neighborhood, there was firewood for the taking.

We stomped down a trail past the Zieglers' place, to the tangle of downed trees in the snowy yard behind it. I'd never met the Zieglers and knew their name only as a label for the large empty summer house perched next to one of our favorite snowshoeing trails. Even in the summer, I'd never seen it occupied. The long-distance call Hig made to ask if we could take the wood was the only time either of us had ever spoken to them.

Empty homes are normal. Seldovia is far enough from the highway-connected world that it's been shrinking for decades. But it's close enough to that world to be marketed as an idyllic summer getaway—a place for summer retreats from Alaska's big city, and from the rest of the country as well. They're easy to spot. Graceful monsters in bright wood with giant picture windows, perched on ocean-view bluffs. No additions wrapped in tattered Tyvek, no litter of broken vehicles in the yard. No gardens. Snowed-in doors. More than half of Seldovia's houses are unoccupied. Vacation homes are often the largest. If anyone measured it, I suspect that most of the square footage of floor space in Seldovia stands empty, nearly all year-round.

We need those empty houses, though—and the image of Seldovia they represent. Our friends build them. Other friends serve meals to day-tripping tourists, or handle the boats that bring tourists back and forth to Homer. The influx of our briefest visitors and part-time residents is an influx of money as well. It drives an annual expansion of community.

Yellow earmuffs on, Hig waded through thigh-deep snow, clambered up the pile of downed trees to chainsaw them into neat cookies. Each round was loaded into the sled, then sent rocketing down the hill to stack in a snow-covered parking lot. The smell of fresh spruce pitch mingled with the acrid gasoline from the chainsaw—both standing out sharply against the odorless world of snow.

We were collecting firewood for Marcella and her family. After they dried, the rounds of spruce would heat their house, reducing reliance on expensive electric heat. Actually, Hig was collecting firewood. I had forgotten how difficult it was to do anything while wearing a baby on front. I had to extend my arms all the way in front of me to pick up anything at all, and lifting something as heavy as one of those wooden cookies was impossible. So I shoved the sled on its way with only a few small limbs inside. I followed it down, contorting to remove the wood, stopping my efforts at a sleepy squeak of protest from Lituya. I rocked back and forth in the snow until a high-pitched whining sent me back up the hill again, where Katmai was launching into a frustrated tirade about the stuck treads on the plastic backhoe he was using to dig at the snow. He looked sleepy as well. I pulled the other wrap out of my fanny pack and soon was wearing both of them again—only slightly lopsided.

I turned to a pile of dried branches instead, loaded them into the sled, tied the prickly mess down with a length of string, and gave the tow rope a tug, starting off down the hill to Marcella's house. These branches wouldn't save anyone money on an electric bill, but they'd build a bonfire to honor Lowell.

Since 1970, the city of Seldovia has shrunk from 437 people to 255. Outside the city limits, the few sprawling miles of road that include our yurt have added 165. The overall numbers have gotten just a little bit smaller with every census. In that same forty years, Homer, on the other side of Kachemak Bay, has grown nearly fivefold, to around five thousand people. It mirrors the pattern of urbanization across the world.

"I don't want to live anywhere connected to the highway system," I had told Hig four years earlier, trudging the sprawling pavement of the first road-connected town we'd seen in months. He had agreed wholeheartedly. That sentiment had become one of our prime criteria for picking a place to live. Of all the towns we'd visited, we loved the disconnected ones most. Lacking an easy connection to the rest of the world seemed to strengthen communities, pushing them into an enforced togetherness that other places can afford to live without. It kept local stores in business—where customers couldn't simply drive farther for a cheaper price. But that isolation from the outside world comes with a lack of job options, dating options, grocery options. We'd chosen Seldovia after a year spent weathering the storms of Alaska in a floorless tent, with an attitude that any life in a permanent heated structure would be unbelievably easy. But the reality of what we've gained and lost in giving up an urban life is more complex.

On my rare visits to Seattle, I notice how I eat more packaged foods (they're cheaper) and how I eat more fruit (also cheaper). I notice how much I enjoy getting a chance to see a movie, or to join a group of people gathered around an obscure and specific interest (like the Japanese martial art of aikido). And I notice how much harder it is to make time for family dinners every day. The togetherness of an isolated town has brought us potatoes and fish and skiff rides and extra hands hanging yurt insulation. It's put us just a quick phone call away from willing partners for fishing adventures or berry-picking trips. Those people love it here too. But the common complaints—about high prices, long winters, the expense of leaving town, and the limitations of the jobs available—are real.

Two years later, two-thirds of the kids in that Friday playgroup would be gone—to nearby Homer and to distant North Carolina. Marcella and her youngest son would move to Homer as well, she to run a bed-and-breakfast and her son to experience the options offered by a larger school. The special-ed aide and his wife would stay in Seldovia less than a year, along with another new family that had arrived at around the same time. Their stories are unique but nearly always follow along familiar lines. Moving toward family or toward larger opportunities. Away from the problems of disconnection.

⌒⌒

The highway from Anchorage to Homer was completed in 1950. Before then, when transportation relied on boats, Seldovia's better harbor made it the local hub and the center of business for the lower Kenai Peninsula. It has a long history for an Alaskan town—put on the map by the Russians in the 1850s, near the site of a more ancient Native encampment. At the turn of the twentieth century, Seldovia was far larger than Anchorage itself, where only a few scattered settlers had put down roots.

It was probably the highway that started the decline. But it was also the earthquake. In 1964, the land drop caused by Alaska's monstrous Good Friday Earthquake flooded the boardwalks Seldovia was built on. In the ensuing struggles over where to rebuild, half the population moved away. Most of the canneries disappeared then as well. And it was also the fisheries. The town's name is based on a Russian word for "Herring Bay." But the herring were fished out of Seldovia in the 1930s, after a 1920s boom that filled the town with Scandinavians.

Hig's family arrived in 1977. His dad, Craig, fished during the tail end of the crab boom. At a glass-topped table in Seldovia's only restaurant, beneath a giant mounted crab on the wall, we listened to some of his stories. Craig told us about pulling crab pots stuffed with too-small crabs, their shell points worn off from measurement after measurement made by other fishermen—measuring them again before tossing them over the side. "Haul them up ten times," he'd said, "and then people wondered why those crabs weren't having babies anymore?!" Gear got faster and faster at pulling up crabs. Crab pots were so numerous you could almost walk to Homer on the buoys. T-shirts were printed for the boat crew: "All we want is a little more than our fair share." Dede chimed in with her stories from packing crab at the last remaining cannery. She'd marveled at the sheer volume of crab coming through, wondering how it could possibly be sustained.

It wasn't. The last cannery closed in Hig's childhood. The tanner crab fishery has been closed since the 1990s, and their numbers are still dismal today. Now Cook Inlet's halibut are in trouble, as are king salmon across the state. As global warming and ocean acidification begin to add their strain to the more direct impacts of nets and hooks, I wonder whether even enlightened fisheries management can be enough. There are only a few fishing boats left that are based in Seldovia. I was here myself for the close of our only full-size grocery store, a holdover from the days when most of the local fleet fed their crews from its shelves. I also witnessed the close of a summer-only restaurant and year-round gift shop.

But I've also seen the opening of a natural food store in the center of town, the arrival of hopeful young newcomers building cabins in the woods, and the start of a community center, yoga classes, and a regular summer craft fair. As I've settled into my life in Seldovia, I find more pieces I can give back myself—giving away bags of extra kale from the garden, helping lead hikes, babysitting Katmai's friends, teaching martial arts, and giving presentations in the school. I see a place bursting with community energy, which might be more important than the census numbers.

If you ask Dede and Craig and the others who've been in Seldovia for thirty years, the story is one of decline. But although the center of town lost about thirty people between the last two censuses, the scattered neighborhoods of hand-built cabins on three- or five-acre lots—the neighborhoods that include us—gained about twenty. Over the same ten years, school enrollment has dipped but only slightly, with enough noise in the numbers that it's hard to see a trend. If you ask the people who've been in Seldovia for ten years, they see something different. They see that people who lived here because they didn't see another option are being replaced by people who live here because they've *chosen* it. People who love our inconvenient paradise.

⤞⤝

Fingers flying over his keyboard, chatting while he worked on lines of computer code, Hig mused that Seldovia would be a great place for high-tech workers. "Just think about it," he said. "They can work from anywhere with internet, and we have good internet. A programmer or consultant could make enough money per hour that they wouldn't even need to work full time to live here. Housing is cheap, they could use subsistence resources, take advantage of all the outdoor opportunities. Life here is awesome. If people only knew about it, we'd have more people than we knew what to do with."

We could use a *few* more. The efficiencies of a village come from its sparseness—room to grow food, local skills replacing a few of the otherwise shipped-in goods, and enough fish, plants, animals, and trees to eat and burn on a sustainable scale. The efficiencies of a city are different—mass transportation and shared apartment walls—and more easily scaled to billions. The world can use both. Plugging our own life into one of the internet's ubiquitous "carbon footprint calculators," we can prove that our impact is better than average. And maybe that helps. But we could do better. And others could do better. None of us could do enough. Carbon dioxide lasts in the atmosphere for centuries. To stabilize global climate— even at a temperature much warmer than today—we need to bring all those footprints down to zero, by reshaping systems much larger than any of us can reach alone. By definition, an unsustainable system must always end. The only question is how.

The paved stripe of the highway to Homer is a technology that's made Seldovia a more isolated place, as stores and services have shifted elsewhere. Better fishing technology can be partially blamed for the crashing fisheries. But cell phones work here now. We watch movies online. Free-shipping Amazon orders offer a plethora of goods far beyond any past or present storefront. Online chats and teleconferences let us collaborate around the world. Can we keep the connection to the modern but regain the sustainability that once supported far more people—for thousands of years—than live here today?

Seldovia's economy, and Alaska's economy, has always been thoroughly tied to the particular resources of this piece of earth. But can the future be untangled from that? Maybe Hig is right. Maybe the future of our little village is computer-geek fishermen, writing code in their hand-built cabins.

10: Beneath the Snow

"THOSE ARE TOES where the dog walked!" Katmai pointed out proudly, squatting down over a particularly clear dog print, placing his mittened thumb inside. Wisps of blond hair poked out of the hood of his bright blue snowsuit. On his feet, he wore felted green booties Dede had sewn for him, their soft soles gripping on the slippery crust. I was always surprised by how well he could walk on the ice.

"What about this one here?" I asked, moving ahead to a track left behind by Dede, the telltale pattern of ice cleats polka-dotting the shape of the boot. But he had already turned away, jabbing the end of a ski pole into the snow with great enthusiasm. Layers of our family's footprints obscured the ski furrows and tread marks of the snow machines beneath—probably nearly a week old by now. On a good weekend powder day, a few of the ski-obsessed Seldovians might pass by the yurt on their way up the hill. On a sunny afternoon, neighborhood snow machiners might come zooming by. Perpendicular to their lines were the deep pockmarks left by snowshoe hares, the tiny handprints of red squirrels, and the eraser-sized tracks of a vole, bounding between hideouts in the nearby bushes and trees.

Snowfall at the yurt

I glanced up from the tracks to see that Katmai, making happy vrooming sounds, was busily shoveling snow into a plastic dump truck. I might daydream about my budding naturalist following animal tracks across the landscape. But for a just-turned-two-year-old, there was no way nature could compete with the allure of heavy machinery. I set to work with my own larger shovel, trying to unearth enough kale for dinner. I've become an evangelist for kale. Sure, it's good for you. Sure, it's tasty and versatile and can work its way happily into pesto and salads and stir-fries and casseroles and soups and kale chips. But, most important, kale loves it here as much as I do.

Sown in the spring, kale balloons into a profusion of curly green, two-foot-tall plants quickly spilling over the edge of the raised beds. It thrives in our cool days and cooler nights, laughs off the early frosts, shakes off an occasional dusting of snow. At the end of the brief summer, when cold and frost turn all else brown and brittle, the kale keeps going. It stands there. Snow covers it. It still stands there. When I dig down to the frozen dirt, the kale's leaves are bent down to the ground from the weight of the snow, ice crystals clinging to their curly fringes—as bright and green as they ever were in August. The ice crystals melt away to reveal a February salad—a perfectly preserved reminder of the buried summer.

Our neighborhood sits on a ridge between Seldovia Bay and Kachemak Bay—both offshoots of the much larger Cook Inlet. Sixteen miles to the southeast, the open Pacific Ocean sits on the other side of a low range of mountains. The closer you get to that ocean, the warmer and wetter the winters (and colder and wetter the summers) are. We sit right in the middle between the massive record-setting snows in Prince William Sound and the drier cold of Anchorage, Fairbanks, and the interior of the state.

My Alaska isn't the Alaska of minus-fifty winters and northern lights streaking across the sky. Temperatures rarely drop below zero Fahrenheit, and dip down into the single digits only a handful of times in an average winter. Blizzards regularly swap places with midwinter thaws, where the air warms to forty degrees and rain melts into the top layer of snow, sinking us thigh-deep in once-solid trails. We get no frostbitten cheeks or hard-core

Alaskan points for winters here. An average day might hover between twenty and thirty degrees. Overcast. And snowing. Looking at weather data, I realized it was as if the Seattle drizzle I'd grown up with had simply been shifted around seventeen degrees colder.

But that seventeen degrees brings an entirely different world.

Shovels, gloves, toys, and buckets. Boats, bicycles, cars, and sheds. Roads and houses. All buried. The world is wiped clean with every snowfall—smooth, perfect, and inaccessible. The bustling busyness of gardens and berries and construction projects fades into a distant-seeming memory as one by one, each time-sucking project disappears beneath the white. The only cars visible are the ones that work well enough to be driven every day. The only doors that open are the ones repeatedly shoveled. The only paths walkable are the ones repeatedly stomped.

Everything else? You'll see it in May. Or maybe June. You probably didn't need it anyway.

Winter encourages minimalism. In summer, hoses and toys are strung out along our driveway. Five-gallon buckets decorate the yard, filled with compost, seaweed, or just-picked carrots. We try to gather them before the snow, piling everything in disorganized heaps in the dirt-walled space beneath the yurt's floor. We forget some. Under the yurt, snow piles in through the open corners, and ice pools in the divots during each freeze cycle, freezing half the rescued items to the ground. Then we go back to rescue them again.

Seldovia doesn't have a snow gauge. But one year, we measured nearly six feet of snow standing on the ground in the middle of March. The drifts at the bottom of the driveway would have buried me with feet to spare. A few times in a winter, they usually do bury something—Dede's van or maybe my bicycle—forcing a treasure hunt by snow shovel.

I stumbled over the skill saw beneath the laundry basket at the foot of the bed, wincing at my stubbed toe, and the seemingly inevitable clutter. Winter reminded me that there was so much we still needed to build here—storage spaces for tools, wood, bicycles, and beets.

But this winter, our water came from a washhouse with a sink, rather than a hole chopped in the ice over our well. This winter, we knew where to get the best firewood. This winter, we had smoothed enough of the bumps out of life in the yurt that I could sink into the rhythms of the world around us. Embracing the snow, from its arrival sometime around Halloween, to the last patches dripping into oblivion sometime around Memorial Day. Enjoying the way the seasons cleaved the year neatly in two: green and white.

I followed my own tracks—sharp outlines of a duck-footed snowshoer on the melted ridges of the snow machine's tread, dog tracks interspersed between them. From the wrap on my back Katmai started telling me a long and rambling story about squirrels, parroting a few of my own explanations.

"Squirrels go *chip chip* and eat seeds from spruce cones. Mama broke spruce cones, and Katmai threw them! And they went down in the snow. And then the squirrels go *chip chip* and eat the seeds!" His words eventually trailed off, his head drooping against my shoulder into an afternoon nap. Lituya was already asleep on my chest.

I stopped to inhale the quiet. Walking in the mist, I could see the glow of the sun behind the thin clouds, and the network of rivulets the last melt had left on the snow's surface. Water dripped from every branch tip, as snow melted into the moist air. It was as peaceful as life could be with two young children. But I was breathing hard from the weight of two heavy warm bodies, slumped in sleep on both sides of my torso. Last time I had weighed them, the kids totaled thirty-five pounds together. Naked. I guessed that their snowsuits added at least another few pounds.

The trail leveled from its relentless climb, avoiding a deep gully by jogging into one of the patches of spruce forest that dotted the alder slope. At sea level, spruce dominates the ecology. Climbing upward, trees are edged out by scrubby thickets of Sitka alder, until at around fifteen hundred feet, both give way to a landscape of tundra. We lived in the middle, at the elevation where alder and spruce interfinger. In late summer, the moss beneath these trees was sprinkled with trailing raspberries, leafy ferns, and bright orange chicken-of-the-woods mushrooms. Now I watched the tracks of rabbits, squirrels, and neighbors, picking out the snowshoe, boot, ski, and dog prints of the half-dozen other users of this piece of wilderness. Occasionally I'd see something special—the craterlike step of a moose or the odd gait of a wolverine. More often, I'd lose myself in disconnected thoughts as my feet followed the familiar path.

This patch of forest was only halfway up the hill—only halfway to what used to be my favorite walk destination. I paused at the edge of the trees, contemplating the interlaced snow machine and snowshoe paths as they climbed the last steep hill ahead of me. But today that last few hundred feet looked daunting. I turned around, carefully using a single ski pole for balance, trying not to trip over feet I couldn't see. I may have smoothed over some of the bumps of life created by cold, dark, and snow. But Lituya was one very big new little bump. The kids outnumbered me now. I had to balance them, not just figuratively but literally—one on each side of my body. Adding a child gave a fresh twist to the same adventure, like the twists Hig and I added to each expedition. Constant adjustment had become my way of life.

I walked back down the trail as if on eggshells, trying to keep each step as smooth as possible to preserve that peaceful slumber, feeling for the edge with the ski pole, dreading the postholes I couldn't see. Katmai was at an awkward transition between napping and not napping. He refused to nap anywhere but on my back. The colorful lengths of fabric that held the two kids to my body were twined and tied around each other. If one woke up crying, they both would.

I had become a three-headed monster.

Somehow I had managed to make it into my thirties without ever owning a car. And I wanted to keep it that way. I had only grudgingly gotten around to getting my driver's license in college, and then promptly found every excuse I could not to use it. Perhaps I hate driving because I learned in Seattle rush-hour traffic. Perhaps I would have hated it anyway. I had managed to get away without getting behind a wheel for years, which provided a good excuse not to drive at all.

Minimizing car trips makes sense. I don't need to bring a hunk of metal that weighs thousands of pounds along with me on every trip. I don't need to burn the fuel—to contribute a few more puffs of carbon dioxide to the atmosphere or to nudge the market toward exploring for dirtier oil in more remote places. I luxuriated in my happy ignorance of car shopping, gas prices, insurance costs, and engine maintenance. Sometimes I ride in cars. For the year we spent walking to the Aleutians, Hig and I stuck to a strict "no motorized transportation" rule. But not here. We join Dede on a town trip once a week for a combined blitz of visiting stores, family, and the dump, repaying the van ride with home-cooked dinners. In the summer, we sometimes join up with friends and family to go fifteen or twenty miles out the road to pick berries, snag salmon, or launch a camping trip. But most of the time, we go under our own power or not at all.

The world's problem with oil addiction and rampant climate change is far bigger than a few three-mile car trips I might or might not make in a given week. Every one of us is part of an unsustainable system so entrenched that individual lifestyle changes cannot possibly get us out of it. Not on their own. But our lives are part of that system. They matter, I hope, at least a little bit. If all my wanderings over melting permafrost, disappearing glaciers, and eroding villages couldn't change me, what could those places do for anyone?

⁌◦⁌

Ice cleats on my feet, on the icy edge of the road, I dreamed of bike trailers.

"You sure you don't want a ride?" a man asked, pulling over in his truck. His face was familiar, one of the Seldovians I knew I ought to know, but I couldn't quite pull up his name.

"No, I'm fine," I smiled. Most people didn't stop to ask anymore. We live "out the road" three miles from Seldovia's main downtown. There is only the one road, with dozens of houses strung out along the main drag and clustered on a handful of side roads. It's always easy to hitch a ride. But by now, people figured I didn't want one. I guessed I didn't. But the kids were getting heavier every day, and I longed for the day Lituya would be big enough that I could use a bike instead of my feet.

"I see you walking with those kids all the time. Guess you like the exercise, huh?"

"Yeah. And it's a good way to get them to sleep. It's not so bad. He's small for his age," I continued dismissively, pointing over my shoulder at Katmai's nodding head. I didn't bring up climate change or sustainability or dependence on fossil fuels. Even if I sometimes felt I should. I didn't even do that with my friends. I never wanted to be *that insufferable greenie.* If people were going to talk about me at all, I preferred the label *oddball adventurer* or simply *tough woman.* Even if I knew it wasn't true. Walking around while carrying a bunch of stuff on your back is the most unskilled task I can imagine. Just one foot in front of the other, a little patience, and anyone will get there eventually. *Tough* implied struggle or some unusual physical gift.

Mostly, I was stubborn. I didn't want a car because I was scared to become dependent on one—to lose the freedom of being able to get my family where it needs to go on muscle power alone. Mostly, I carry them to get us out into the great outdoors.

∽◦

I ducked carefully under the boughs of the tree where I'd propped up my snowshoes, trying to grab them without setting loose an avalanche on me or Lituya. Nearly asleep already, her small head poked above the zipper of my once-yellow raincoat. Over the past twenty-four hours, around a foot of snow had fallen. The still air had left wet pillows perched precariously on every branch and twig. Spruce limbs bowed beneath the weight of it all— drooping over the wood-splitting station and the path, brushing our heads.

Retrieved now, my snowshoes made a furrow in knee-deep snow, following the furrow left by our dog Panda's belly. Hig followed me, aiming each step right between my own to smooth the trail, while Katmai conversed in a series of exclamation points from his back. "Go to the TV tower trail!"

All the trails had disappeared beneath the fresh snow, and I turned sideways, choosing a new path. Between May and November, we rarely venture beyond the network of trails that lace Seldovia's thick and thorny jungle. Winter is different. With the right pattern of snowfalls, the alders bow down toward the ground under the weight of snow, then freeze where they lie, turning a thicket of ten-foot-tall brush into a smooth field of white. Sometimes we wait the whole winter for them to be buried. Sometimes it happens in November.

It was February, and in this particular year, most of the alder had been down for months. With my ski pole, I thwacked a pair that weren't. They loosed their load of snow with a shudder, clearing a way for me to walk underneath. A few snowflakes wormed their way into my clothes, leaving cold drops on Lituya's downy red hair. The snow began to fall again, white flakes fluttering from a white sky, forming perfect crystalline stars on the folds of my coat.

Katmai craned his head as far back as Hig's wrap would let him, mouth open. "You are eating snowflakes!"

With squeaks and wiggles, Lituya began to stir. "Hang on," I said. "I think she needs to nurse." Hig snowshoed around me, taking up the trail-breaking position. I loosened a knot in the wrap, then pulled and tugged at the various bits of fabric, reaching underneath to adjust my shirt and Lituya's head, trying to close the few-inch gap that separated her mouth from my nipple. Finally, I got her arranged, zipped my coat up again, and continued to where Hig was waiting a few yards ahead.

"Nursing while snowshoeing!" I proclaimed proudly. "I never managed that with Katmai."

"That's great," Hig said, tromping on.

"Hang on, slow down a little. If I go too fast, I'm worried I might dislodge her."

Panda, tired of breaking trail, fell in behind me, her front paws stepping on the backs of my snowshoes. I wasn't sure where we were going. It didn't matter. The snow opened up the world, giving us access to a million tiny places we've never been. And the snow equalized the world, papering over the differences between the ecosystems beneath it. The details that remained stood out even more starkly. Meadows and thickets were a bright smooth white. The forests were dark and shadowed, with only a scant foot of snow over their downed logs and dropped branches. The sun—even in its brief and weakened winter form—heats the dark-colored spruce branches enough to melt the snow. Enough that most of it never reaches the ground beneath the trees.

We paused beneath a tree we'd come to call the "weeping spruce." The trees here belong to only one species but bear a remarkable variety of shapes. Each silhouette is a personality. Some have short stubby branches, reaching toward the sky like oversized bottle brushes. Some have branches that sweep up at the tips, while others droop like the fur of a shaggy dog. Some sport straight branches in a perfect Christmas-tree cone. This particular spruce resembled a bristly weeping willow, with branches that hung straight down—sometimes twenty vertical feet—and swung in the wind like a beaded curtain.

The tree was our own tiny discovery, only a mile or two from home. I collected these discoveries. Each one was a secret morsel of knowledge that we could keep or share with our neighbors. Each discovery was one more thread of experience connecting us to this place. The wide hulk of a "grandmother" tree with thick gnarled branches begging to be climbed. A truck-sized boulder dropped by a glacier and buried in ferns. A hilltop decorated in rare wild crabapples. A meadow of cranberries and orchids. A snag sporting chicken-of-the-woods mushrooms.

It was the first time we'd come this way all winter, along a route we'd pioneered and had once regularly stomped. The winter before, the three of us had gotten out twice as often and wandered twice as far. With four now, the circle we could easily travel had shrunk, and the time had become harder to find. Lituya had fallen asleep again, and I unzipped my coat, trying to rearrange her into a more comfortable position. Katmai was asleep as well. Even here, where it is six months long, winter is only a moment in time.

Having a two-year-old and a six-week-old was bound to be a moment in time as well. It was a brand-new hurdle growing easier with every outing.

"We should do this more often."

"We will."

11: The Smallest Adventure

I VANISHED A FEW STEPS into the bushes, wiggling my rubber boot to find purchase between the slippery salmonberry canes. My elbows deflected the branches, setting loose a shower of leaf-caught rain. A five-gallon bucket—bearing the faded logo of the kitty litter it once contained—dangled from one hand. Deep in the thicket, I stared up at the tri-part salmonberry leaves, drips hanging from their pointed tips, serrated edges cutting a jagged puzzle of the sky. Backlit berries glowed vermillion against the dripping gray. A few were nearly black with ripeness. A few were a burst of orange and gold. In the bucket, the bottom layers were slowly being crushed by their own weight, into a pulp of soft seedy flesh and ruby juice that resembled the jam they would become.

I was sopping wet. The sleeves of my cotton sweatshirt dripped like sponges and felt as heavy as bricks, poking out through the cuffs of last summer's worn-out raingear. In its yellowish wrinkles, I could pick out bushwhacking tears from our trip through Chuitna, fire holes from Usibelli, and peeling waterproofing from weeks of continuous wear in the Arctic. Water ran in through the seams on my shoulders, accumulating in a sodden mass around my wrists and waist. I rolled up my cuffs, balanced

Fresh salmonberries plucked around the yurt, baked into a mouth-watering pie the bucket on a clearish patch of ground, opened its lid, and continued my picking.

It didn't matter if I was wet. Being wet only matters if you're likely to be hypothermic. It was early August, with temperatures warm in the fifties. I was picking about two yards from my own driveway, halfway between the yurt and Dede's house. Dry clothes were infinite and available, and I could bother with them later. It felt like a privilege not to care.

Down the hill from the salmonberry thicket, a few silver drops clung to the blueberries' oval leaves. Branches drooped to the ground, heavy with clusters of plump berries that had just gained their opaque blush of ripeness. On the driveway above me, Katmai scooted back and forth on his tiny pedal-less bike as Dede cheered him on. He detoured to eat every ripe strawberry (and a few unripe ones) from the plants that lined the path. Lituya sat in the grass, fleece suit staining green and brown as she explored the leaves.

Hig crashed by in the brush a few yards away, and I brandished my berry picker in excitement. "I can't believe we missed these bushes all those other years. They're not even fifty feet from the driveway, and I never even knew they were here! And they're so awesome. Look how full this bucket is! I'll never finish picking them all by dinnertime."

"That's pretty impressive," Hig said offhandedly, glancing into my bucket as he climbed the hill with an armful of devil's club stalks. He might have sounded more impressed if I hadn't said the same thing yesterday afternoon when I'd first found these bushes, and at least one or two other times within the past few hours.

"If you join me now, I bet we can clean out this patch."

"I'm doing stuff," he replied, gesturing to the devil's club he'd been clearing.

I wanted the help but could hardly object to the murder of devil's club. Fewer festering spines, more room for berry bushes to grow—more berries to pick next year.

Hig and I split child care, collaborate on work, and cherish our family hikes. Beyond that, we find ourselves channeled into parallel paths worn deeper with each passing year. The garden is my baby, the berry patches my treasures, and the kitchen my domain. The chainsaw belongs firmly to Hig, along with the associated firewood piles, power tools, and the sewing machine. But I can pick more than enough berries for both of us. My eyes focus to a well-honed precision, straining to glimpse glints of red or blue between the distractions of leaves and branches, as I scan my horizons for promising picking grounds. I bend to the ground, lifting up branches from the shadows of ferns and fireweed, looking for those hidden twigs held down by the weight of their fruit. The metal comb of the berry picker plucks blueberries from their stems a dozen at a time, improving efficiency over the stumbling slowness of human fingers.

Unless I fight the impulse, I soon find that I see literally nothing else. Not the sparrows rustling the bushes beside me, the eagles overhead, the cars on the road below, or the plants that grow no edible pieces. Hours disappear, while I fill and fill until my bucket literally cannot hold any more, fingers purple, baby hungry, and the rest of my family impatient. My back aches from bending. Images of blueberries burn my eyelids when I lay down to sleep—and dream of berries.

Nearly every part of Alaska is abundant in berries—cloudberries and nagoonberries, crowberries and salmonberries, cranberries and blueberries. But I can't blame my surroundings for my obsession. I was always like this. In Seattle, I would set out on bike expeditions halfway across the city, filling tubs and ziplocks with the Himalayan blackberries that grew to engulf any untended patch of land, my hands stained red with juice and scratches, barely able to pedal home under the weight of all that fruit. Most people just picked a handful or two as they walked past. Most people probably thought I was weird.

The Seattle metro area has about ten thousand times Seldovia's population, but berry picking here is more competitive. Filling one's freezer with berries is an every-summer ritual, and blueberries are the most prized crop. Around Solstice, the soundtrack of summer begins with the whine of mosquitoes. As July turns to August, the disappearing bugs are slowly drowned out by an increasingly incessant barking. Every night, sometimes all night. From Dede's porch I hear a series of short staccato barks, then the rushing scrabble of claws on gravel as Panda erupts down the driveway, volume increasing as she races past our thin fabric walls to the lookout over the clearcut, defending her territory with a deafening bravado that belies her cowardly nature. Summer starts at the ocean, rising up the hills as ripe berries give way to green ones, then to flowers, and finally to the lingering patches of snow. When everything is ripe at our elevation, we are suddenly surrounded by bears.

On the south side of Kachemak Bay, black bears are the only bears we have. They're common throughout the season they're awake, leaving footprints and scat in the mud of our trails. We might see a black rump fleeing ahead of a car, a pair of black ears above a meal of devil's club berries, or claws gripping bark—treed by a dog. There are no stories of violence from our local bear population—only tales of mysteriously disappeared bags of garden lime, chewed-up bike seats, devoured chickens, and paw prints on window glass.

Dede never trained Panda for much. But as a puppy, she held her up to the window when a bear was on the porch, impressing upon the terrified pup the importance of that lumbering giant. Bear guard is Panda's single trick. I am used to sleeping through her barks, both grateful and surprised that the bears respect her territory. But that respect extends to structures, gardens, and the driveway only. Berry bushes are fair game. While I checked their ripeness every day, the bears did the same nearly every night.

~⁄○

After a feast of blueberry muffins, currant scones, and quickly gulped coffee, we headed back out into the bushes for the third day of our week-long project. This wasn't just a few days of berry picking. This was a full-scale *project*—vacation email message turned on, plans made, and all other commitments canceled for the week. We planned to have the smallest adventure we could possibly imagine—one week within an eighth of a mile of the yurt. With the project came a set of self-imposed rules. We refused to set foot outside the boundaries we'd drawn. We committed to spend our days outside and refused to do any work unrelated to our exploration.

The berries provided the excuse. Gathering food was a clearly utilitarian pursuit, and a fine thing to structure a week of activities around, but we had broader goals. This project would let us play backyard scientists, drawing maps of all the ecosystems around our yurt, learning new plants and animals, following the complicated geography, learning where (and why) the best berries grew. Katmai (now two and a half) could become a regular little naturalist! At six months, Lituya could ride on my back. We could visit places walled off by thick enough brush that I'd never even stood there. Surely we'd learn something; surely we'd notice things we'd never seen before.

A friend called it our backyard vacation. I bristled a bit at the characterization. We were *doing things*! Doing things like sharing sandwiches with a friend and her two kids in a patch of moss in the dappled shade of a pair of spruce trees, berry buckets half-full beside us, watching butterflies. I grabbed the camera, wanting a picture to add to Hig's growing catalog of all the insects and spiders in the area.

It was a vacation and a project. As self-employed yurt-dwellers, our daily work and home and social lives blended together in a great jumble of laptops, stuffed animals, and berry pies. But ever since we'd first set off on our first major wilderness expedition, our life had been punctuated by journeys and projects—anchoring memories and defining the structure of our years. I needed the rules. I needed the language of a project and its ambitious goals to give myself the space to dive into something we normally could only spare scattered bits of time for.

Our eighth-mile circle extended beyond the bounds of our three-acre property, to include neighboring clearcuts and a few neighboring houses. But most of the people we saw were the guests who came to visit us.

"Here, walk with me. You have to try *our* salmonberries."

I strolled up the first few yards of the TV tower trail, seeking a few fresh berries to complete my salmonberry pie. My friend Ellis followed a few steps behind me, reaching out to pick a likely red fruit. "They aren't quite as good as yours to eat fresh," I admitted. "But they do make an awesome pie and jam." One year earlier and 750 miles away, we'd sat with Ellis and Art in their Point Hope home, eating bowls of cloudberries and granola, and marveling over their creations. Art carved intricate masks, adding his own spark to thousands of years of Point Hope history. Ellis looked in as an outsider, photographing whaling and everyday life. He's from Point Hope. She's from Amsterdam. Their new baby spanned a gulf of half the world. Their visit to us completed a circle of hospitality.

But on this night, fifteen people crowded into our yurt for dinner. I gathered up nearly all the plates from our mostly handmade and mismatched set, empty canning jars serving as water glasses. The guests came from all corners—not just Point Hope and Amsterdam but Seldovia, Homer, and Texas. On one side of the room, Ellis held a lively conversation in Dutch with a longtime Seldovian who'd originally come from Holland. On the other side, Art uncovered mutual friends with our visitors from Homer. In between, two toddlers and two babies created a comfortable background of cheerful noise and chaos.

Refusing to venture more than a few minutes' walk from home, I expected a measure of social isolation. Instead, the people came to us—not just these guests, but seven others besides on other days—from all over the state, country, and world. This turning of the tables struck me as a perfect expression of our odd little adventure. From distant grandeur to intimate exploration. From grateful bums to gracious hosts. In so many villages, towns, and homesteads, people have opened their doors to us. We wander in, grubby and hungry, fed and warmed by total strangers, growing close to an array of people we would never have met otherwise.

This time, I fed a pile of visitors—from our bushes—with salmonberry pie, blueberry muffins, currant scones, rhubarb-currant cake, and blueberry cobbler. And from our garden—with broccoli, kale, cabbages, beets, kohlrabi, and greens in an ever-shifting combination of stir-fries and salads.

Deep in the clearcut, Katmai crawled into a tunnel in the head-high grass, peering out at Lituya, who watched, laughing, from a perch just outside of the soggy meadow. Hig snapped a photo of me with my clipboard, looking official as I jotted down a list of all the plants I could see around me. Then he stared at our little GPS, picking out our next destination.

The screen showed us that the yurt was 150 yards away. It seemed much farther. This slope—part of the clearcut that bordered our land— was one of the many places that we blithely snowshoed over in the winter but had never dared to visit when summer exploded over the stumbling, foot-trapping logging slash. An occasional startling glance showed me a corner of the yurt's brown roof, through a screen of alder leaves and fire-weed blooms.

Here, currant bushes cascade over silvery spruce stumps, between patches of devil's club, canes of salmonberries, and the secret gems of blue-berry bushes. A few stragglers and snags of spruce still tower above the thicket, left behind when it was logged about ten years back. Between them, a miniature forest of young pines and larches is growing—planted to replace the native spruce monoculture with something alternative—something the Seldovia Native Association hopes will be profitable to log one day.

The Native Association owns a large chunk of land in the area. Much of it is logged, with clearcut patches new and old scattered all along Seldovia's couple dozen miles of road. Along with the Seldovia Village Tribe, the Native Association is a big part of the town's economy and power structure. Between the two, they have cut trees, sold berry jam to tourists, run a gift shop and a clinic, organized teen movie nights and a toddler play group, built and piloted a ferry, and received grants for any number of proj-ects both sensible and impractical.

❧

The forest that was cut here was virgin old-growth. But it wasn't the tower-ing mossy giants that those words bring to mind. Here, even the oldest trees are only a few feet in diameter. And every single one of them is a spruce tree.

Seldovia is at the rainforest's ragged northern edge, where it gives way to the boreal forest of the northern interior. Trees grow slowly here. Even with the planted imports, this forest will probably not be logged again in my lifetime. It will be decades before we can even call it a forest again. Logging once is easy. But to log sustainably would be to log on a time scale impractically small or unfeasibly slow for any large-scale export operation.

As we let the GPS define our wandering path, I watched for the little pines and larches, noting which ones survived another winter and how quickly they're growing. They're alien invaders. They're pioneers. They're an experiment I can watch from my doorstep. As the climate warms around us, I wonder if they will come to own this patch of land, or if the native spruce will eventually take over. So far, the newcomers are winning. Will the kids bring their children here to pick blueberries, in the gaps between still-sparse trees? Or to wander beneath the dappled shade of a larch and pine forest? Or to walk the roads and driveways of another neighborhood of summer homes?

Hig and I picked up the kids, strapped them onto our backs, and set off through the tangle. One of Katmai's rubber boots fell off in the brush, never to be found again.

～⁄～

Our driveway marks the boundary between the original and the disturbed. On one side, our gardens and paths butt up against the edge of our land and the clearcut beyond. On the other side, faint bear trails behind the yurt link up small islands of spruce forest, weaving through tangles of Sitka alder on their way up the mountains.

A spring bubbled up beneath the spiny platters of devil's club leaves. Moss sheared off the rock beneath my foot. I squeezed through sharp-needled branches, green glowing across my eyes as they adjusted to a sudden darkness. Ahead of me, Hig's steps were soft on fallen needles, punctuated by the cracks of shattering twigs.

At the southeastern edge of this patch of forest, huge branches swept a floor-length curtain to the brush. Around the rest of the circle those sweeping branches were dead and rotting, crowded out by an outer ring of new young trees. The forest was pushing out into the brush, taking over the hillside from the alder that surrounded it. Old photos of Seldovia show some of our forests before they were logged. Even older photos show some of them before they were grown—thickets or grass where we now see towering trees. Just a few hundred years ago, there probably weren't many trees at this elevation. Seldovia is the end of the rainforest's range, where small shifts in climate have large consequences on exactly where trees can grow. Cold periods favor meadows, and warmer ones forests. And all of Alaska is getting warmer fast.

Bottom in the air, feet and face both buried in spruce cones, Katmai attempted to climb into the fist-sized hole made by a red squirrel. His pants, sweater, socks, and hair were all speckled with the brown confetti of dismantled cones. Lituya watched, concentrating on picking up spruce cones in her still-awkward fists. Overhead, squirrels chattered angrily at our intrusion. The kids were sitting on top of a "squirrel castle"—a huge mound of spruce cone litter left by generations of squirrels rooting for the seeds inside them, pockmarked with squirrel-sized holes. I walked as far away as I dared, trying to watch without the kids noticing me. Trying to photograph what looked to me like magic.

I'd chosen this project for the children. Not because they needed the rules and boundaries and enforced closing of the laptops to play outside. But because I wanted to try and see this piece of land from a kid's point of view. I wanted to imagine growing up as a child here myself. With bugs and bears and thick and thorny undergrowth, our forests couldn't quite be the tame European woods of *Winnie the Pooh*. But they were too close and too friendly for *Hansel and Gretel* or *Little Red Riding Hood*.

The evening before, I'd shuffled through the mixed-up chaos of the kids' bookshelf, searching out *Blueberries for Sal* by Robert McCloskey. As Katmai curled up in my lap to listen, I was struck by how much his days were just like Sal's—right down to the clearcut stumps in the berry field, the ragamuffin clothing and hairdo, the impatience of a child trying to eat the berries out of mother's pail while I tried to preserve them for the winter. Everything except the mother bear and cub. Even the bears were out there somewhere. I always read growing-up-in-the-woods stories with a little romanticized longing. What would it be like as a kid to have wilderness at your doorstep? To just wander outside into a world with no fences, beyond the sight of any house?

Between filling the berry buckets, Hig and I picked up clippers and saws, cutting short and meandering "explorer trails" through our land, designing paths for tiny feet, wondering how long it would be before they could walk them without us. Will the fallen logs become secret castles for fairies and gnomes? Will there be tree forts and hide-and-seek and kingdoms beyond the reach of grownups? Will they wander off into the woods with a friend and a dog, discovering special little places I've never been myself?

Or not. Maybe I'm just trying to give our children what I kind of wish I'd had, ignoring all the things I took for granted. The things we're not giving them. Like an infinite array of organized kids' activities and more than a handful of same-age peers. Like a toilet. Like cheap oil. Like a stable global climate.

12: Planning the Improbable

FALLING RAIN IS LOUD on the vinyl roof of the yurt—almost as loud as in a tent. Its spatter drowned out the quiet radio. Rivulets of water ran down the skylight and across the windows, stretching into elongate drops. The basil plants on the windowsill craned their stems toward the glass, trying to catch a nonexistent flash of sun. It was the middle of August. Four weeks until our next expedition. The third straight day of pouring rain. I watched the drips as I nursed a mug of coffee, enjoying the rare morning where I woke before the kids. My first thought was: "I guess I don't need to water the garden." Then: "What possessed me to plan an expedition where we can expect this kind of weather *all the time*?" And finally: "Maybe this is a good day to test rain suits."

Our plan, at this point, seemed even more absurd than when we'd dreamed it up a year earlier. It seemed complicated, fascinating, difficult, exciting, unpleasant, amazing, and possibly unsuccessful. I'd spent a year forgetting the rain, remembering instead the moments of discovery and the feeling of awe at whatever the world might bring. Even when it brings nothing but water.

Testing Katmai's raingear while harvesting from the garden on a wet August day

Which might explain why we were planning to spend two of the wettest months of the year in one of the wetter places on the planet: on the vast icy lobe of Malaspina Glacier.

‿○

Katmai stomped in tire-rut puddles as I harvested an excess of kale to pawn off on some nongardening neighbors. His lurid pink rain suit glowed against the wet green and muddy brown. It wasn't leaking. Yet. Lituya sat in a puddle next to the last remaining giant kohlrabi, in a bright yellow rain suit of her own. My own raincoat could more accurately be described as a battered piece of fabric used solely for the psychological benefit of feeling like I dressed for the weather. Sewing raingear for the adults was one of the tasks yet to be erased from our seemingly infinite list, crowded in a multicolored jumble on a white board that hung from the lattice of the yurt.

We had dreamed up this expedition before we even knew who was coming. When Lituya was an unnamed grapefruit-sized creature curled inside her amniotic fluid, I already had her first adventure planned. The seeds of the idea had been planted years before that. By two wet and hungry people, a hundred miles from anywhere, wishing we had spare food enough to explore.

Malaspina Glacier is part of Alaska's Lost Coast, my favorite terrible place in the world. "Lost" because even for Alaska, this stretch of shoreline is harsh, remote, and lacking both harbors and human habitation. On this four-hundred-mile stretch between Glacier Bay and Prince William Sound, only the small village of Yakutat interrupts the wild shore. Giant peaks of the Saint Elias Range rise almost straight from the ocean, creating some of the highest relief in the world. Flowing down from their snowy icefields, North America's largest glaciers spill onto the beach plain in huge, rapidly melting lobes. Storms whipped up in the Aleutians whirl down the coastline, funneled onto the narrow strip of beaches between the roiling ocean and the towering peaks. The landscapes of the Lost Coast are like nothing we've seen anywhere. When it is awful, it's the most desolate place on earth. When it is gorgeous, there's no place as stunning. And at all the moments in between, its scale simply dwarfs us.

Four years ago, the two months of short days, cold sleet, and howling wind we'd spent on these shores marked the midpoint of our yearlong journey. It was nothing more than another piece of wilderness, but it was the inflection point of our lives. The point where we decided to have our first child. The point where I became an Alaskan for good. The point where our former life faded to irrelevance, and I knew we would never go back.

All our expeditions spring from shared dreams—from late-night conversations by a crackling woodstove, tossing outlandish ideas back and forth, then rushing over to the computer to huddle together over the magical possibilities presented by a Google Earth screen. But this one owed more than a little bit to Hig the Geologist.

In a satellite image, Malaspina Glacier is a pair of white bulbs that span a width of forty miles, their necks narrowing into a tumble of crevasses as they pass through a range of impossibly high peaks, to the even larger expanse of barren ice behind them. At the glacier's wrinkled edges, the white turns to gray, and then to green, as the ice is covered first by rocks and mud, then by entire forests, where crevasses rend the ground and send uprooted trees into the abyss. Deep in the middle of the icy lobes, a twelve-mile-long range of mountains lies hidden, surrounded entirely by ice. Glaciers are always dynamic places. But in this era of rapid warming, that dynamism has been speeded up to a scale that we can watch—in real time.

Whatever their original purpose, all our journeys became journeys into climate change. We walked through it everywhere. In the tight-spaced trunks of an expanding patch of spruce trees, the soft new ground under a glacier's shrunken snout, the mud beneath a cliff of crumbling permafrost, a sinkhole in the beach, a dried-out swamp, a tangle of beetle-killed spruce, or a jungle of willows where tundra used to be. We'd listened to the fear in the voice of a Kivalina elder as he ran through the litany of changes and problems that appeared "when the global warming came."

We hoped Malaspina would be the place where all our scattered observations would come together. In this hulking low-elevation glacier, the story of climate change promised to be even more obvious and dramatic than everything we'd seen before. Its shifting and melting would *be* the landscape. No one lives on the glacier's melting bluffs and eroding shores. I would miss that human connection. But maybe it was a good thing. Malaspina would be a place where we could step back for a moment, to watch climate change without the complicated mix of fear and sadness that comes from seeing that change encroaching on human settlements and human traditions.

❧

I pored over Israel C. Russell's hand-drawn maps, archaic spellings, and flowery language—evoking a sense of wonder missing from most modern scientific papers.

> *Its surface, when not concealed by moraines, is broadly undulating, and recalls the appearance of the rolling prairie lands west of the Mississippi. From the higher swells on its surface one may see for many miles in all directions without observing a single object to break the monotony of the frozen plain. So vast is the glacier that, on looking down on it from elevations of two or three thousand feet above its surface, its limits are beyond the reach of vision.*
> *—Israel C. Russell, 1893*

In 1890, funded by the very first grant the National Geographic Society ever gave, Russell set out to explore this icy unknown. I lingered over his descriptions of upside-down lakes, yawning pits, and erupting springs, adding them to my own memories of forests grown on a surface of ice. In a few short weeks, Hig and I and our kids would be lucky enough to touch down in this world.

At least, I tried to think of it as "lucky," pulling my brain free, for a moment, from the crush of logistics and last-minute worries. Here, Russell's words added dramatic specificity to my generic concerns about bears, weather, and ice conditions.

> *The sides of such ridges are exceedingly difficult to climb, owing to the looseness of the stones, which slide from beneath one's feet and roll down the slopes.*
>
> *. . . the melting of the ice beneath the vegetation has left concealed pit-falls into which one may drop without warning.*

. . . there are large quantities of tenacious clay, filled with angular stones, which is so soft, especially during heavy rains, that one may sink waist deep in the treacherous mass. Sometimes blocks of stone a foot or more square float on the liquid mud and lure the unwary traveler to disaster.
—*Israel C. Russell, 1893*

I like to think of myself as a wary traveler. And while I expected our cautious approach to protect against the lure to disaster, it gave us no guarantee we could actually do what we were aiming to. Our plan began in the ice-locked Samovar Hills, hidden deep within the body of the glacier. From there, we would make our way across the vast lobe of ice, through a jumbled forest growing on the glacier's edge, then around it on a wave-swept coast. Day hikes excluded, we only needed to cover around a hundred miles in the two months we had allotted. A hundred miles of deep and trail-less wilderness, with no human presence beyond what we would bring. Through two months of dark and stormy autumn.

Other adventurers travel this coast sometimes. Backpackers have explored the Samovar Hills. Climbers have scaled the giants of the Saint Elias Range. In 1897, the Duke of Abruzzi led an expedition across the other side of the glacier to climb Mount Saint Elias. But for some of our hundred miles—across the ice sheet itself—we could find no record of any travelers since Russell's own expeditions.

I found an old photo of Russell's team, where five bearded men rested on a field of sharp cobbles and boulders, long staffs in hand. Their pots hung awkwardly from backpacks held together with a lashing of twine, stern expressions on every face, looking like the epitome of explorers in grainy black and white.

In our own expedition team photo, Hig and I stood in the garden, lumpy packs bulging from our backs, holding in the fussing children trying to wiggle their way out of the wraps on our chests. Our qualifications spanned the range from PhD-level skills in sedimentary geology to learning-to-crawl skills in sediment eating. We'd planned for the middle of nowhere before. But here, the middle of nowhere collided with harsh weather, unknowable terrain, and a stretch of time four times longer than we'd ever spent entirely in the wild. And our expedition team included an eight-month-old baby who couldn't yet walk, and a two-and-a-half-year-old toddler who walked only in wandering circles between streams and bugs and climbing rocks. Despite our best efforts, neither were potty trained.

≈

I dressed Lituya in a turquoise diaper, holding a red diaper, posing in front of a teetering stack of diaper packages, each one featuring a smiling diaper-clad baby of its own. Each plastic package contained thirty-two white paper pads—compostable inserts to fill those colorful cloth diapers—four per day for the smaller kid and three per day for the larger one, for a grand total of 427 diaper pads. Those 427 could be buried or burned. The half-dozen cloth covers would have to be washed—I hoped not too often. I supposed I was lucky they could, just barely, share a size. Diapers are harder to ration than food. Running short of food was at least a familiar discomfort. We never planned to be hungry. But if we were, we could simply feed the kids first. Running short of diapers was a rather more disgusting proposition.

I left the diapers to return to the pile on the bed, where Katmai stood, still in his pajamas, puzzling over an AA battery charger. The latest set of gifts from the post office had been opened and unceremoniously dumped on the rumpled covers, consisting this day of coconut oil, a bicycle wheel, electric fencing, waterproof paper, lightweight string, and the battery charger. Each day brought a few more boxes, the fruits of last-minute online ordering, with a few gifts from sponsors mixed in. I guessed that our trip was probably the only glacier expedition ever to be sponsored by a diaper company.

Our old baby scale—acquired for hiking gear long before we ever had a baby—emerged from its dusty home beneath the bed. Everything we might need was sorted and weighed and entered into a spreadsheet, the staggering sum sparking a series of fervent discussions where we tried to figure out some way we could leave some object behind, then realizing there was yet another item we forgot. A packraft to fit the whole family, six pounds. Tent with an internal stove, six pounds. Kid life vests, half a pound each. I weighed the kids too. They were about forty-five pounds in total, and inching up every day.

The lead-up to this expedition was a swirling blend of excitement and stress familiar from every expedition past, the emotions seesawing in prominence by the hour or the day. In half my brain, I held a vivid image of climbing on boulders with Katmai, listening to the bellows of hauled-out sea lions as the sun rose over the surf. In the other half, I held an equally vivid image of attempting to shove a dry bag full of diapers into an overstuffed pack in the pouring rain, as two children howled with tears and we scrambled to move camp to any spot away from the bear trails. In details, both scenes were imaginary. In essence, both were likely to come true.

The arc of this journey sprung from our inspiration. But the details sprung from our limitations, and as our plans unfolded, they presented a set of challenges we'd never seen before, solutions leading to problems needing solutions, miring us in a vicious loop it seemed we might never break out of. Extending into November, this trip promised harsher weather than we'd seen in our Arctic journey. On the nastiest days, we could no longer rely on packing up quickly and walking all day long to stay warm. We'd never pack fast enough. And the kids, not walking themselves, wouldn't be warm.

So we planned to carry a tent with a woodstove—a heavier base camp we could leave up for several days at a stretch. But a longer-term camp needs better protection from curious bears, so we bought a portable electric fence. Similar to a fence designed for livestock, these wires can be strung around a tent or campsite, operate on a pair of AA batteries, and give a brief but intense shock to a probing nose or paw. Safe enough not to harm a child, powerful enough to drive back a bear. Weighing barely more than a pound, they sounded too good to be true, but rangers and bear-viewing guides in Katmai National Park swear by them. The evidence was solid.

For two months, we wouldn't see the inside of a single building. All our food and diaper pads would have to be resupplied via pre-hung caches, which must also be protected from bears. All of our technology—including a satellite phone, multiple cameras, and the batteries for the bear fence—

would have to be charged via a tangle of wires, connectors, and a folding solar panel attached to the outside of a pack. Every single one of these things added weight to our still-imaginary packs. Until the whole idea of moving at all, even five miles a day, seemed like an insurmountable obstacle.

The bicycle wheel resting on the bed was the centerpiece of an as-yet-minimally-tested plan involving a wheelbarrow-like cart constructed of willow saplings and a packraft, which we could theoretically maneuver over the rocky undulating surface of a glacier we'd never seen, which could theoretically be anything from a sidewalk of ice to a steep slope of unstable boulders. Maybe Katmai could ride in this cart, if we managed to build it from the wood available in the Samovar Hills (which we'd also never seen). Maybe the kids would ride on our backs, while we pushed and pulled our gear in the cart. Maybe the bicycle wheel would prove just one more piece of gear to lug in our overstuffed backpacks while the kids dangled heavily from wraps on our chests, obscuring the vision of boulders beneath our feet.

I envisioned each image in turn, finding each one oddly amusing. I didn't just dread the potential difficulties—I also looked forward to them. In the catalog of memory, images of stunning wildlife and expansive vistas run head to head with nearly impenetrable bushwhacks, buried tents, apocalyptic windstorms, and gear cleverly repaired with dental floss and glue. The latter set I recall with an unlikely fondness, each one expendable, but as a whole, utterly crucial to that elusive and addictive quality of adventure.

Adventure is a mistake one makes on purpose. It springs from a naive optimism that we can, in fact, do something that seems impossible, and from the stubborn perseverance to make it actually happen. It's a sense of being faced with obstacles you're not quite sure you can overcome. It's eagerly anticipated unknowns and never-anticipated problems. Adventure is pushing our own limits from wherever we left them last time, toeing the line between challenge and imprudence. With stubbornness we cultivate flexibility. Within the bounds of caution, we explore creativity. Along with patience, we need guts.

☙

The bucket fell into the devil's club with a crash, spilling a little of its heavy load of sand, bending beyond recognition the tiny carabiner that (hadn't) held it. On my back, Lituya stirred a little in her slumber.

"I guess the third time isn't the charm either!" I yelled up to Hig.

"I'm going to come down now—I need to rethink the system before we try again! Maybe this string isn't going to work!" Hig was perched high in a spruce tree behind the washhouse, working a system of strings and pulleys, trying to figure out the most stripped-down method possible to hang forty to a hundred pounds of food from a tree, out of the reach of bears. We'd need to set three of these caches on our way out to our start point, our chartered plane hopping from beach to beach with only a brief window to accomplish the task. We were depending on this food to be there for us, intact, up to a month and a half later. It seemed important enough that we ought to have figured it out earlier.

I left him climbing down and headed back to the washhouse porch, where I was testing the solar charging system for our camera. Katmai was as interested in dismantling it as I was in testing it, so I rounded him up and headed back inside. After nursing the now-awake Lituya, getting Katmai some bread and jam, refereeing a fight over a stuffed animal, and making myself another cup of coffee, I didn't actually remember what I'd come in for. I glanced at the crowded to-do list, sure there was something I'd been meaning to add. Then I waded through the ankle-deep scraps of nylon, fleece, and broken rubber bands (used to replace the missing belt in our old sewing machine—a lime-green garage-sale find with the approximate weight of an anvil) that littered our floor from Hig's latest sewing projects. I attempted to load my pack.

The homemade dry bag containing all our sleeping bags was inexplicably taller than the pack it needed to go in, its rolled clip sticking several inches beyond the upper cinch string. Reaching down into the crevices around it, I fit six days' worth of diaper pads, then started to fill the gaps with assorted pieces of gear organized solely by size and shape. A gallon aluminum pot and a pair of kid life vests hung from the outside on an assortment of straps.

The misshapen reality of the pack—little more than a sack with straps—and the pile of not-fitting gear beside it bore little resemblance to the neat columns of items and weights on our spreadsheet. And there was basically no room left for food. I turned to the list, added "expand pack," and scanned through it again, hoping I'd find something I could erase. Then I went out to try the bear fence.

Two weeks later, we began by contemplating failure. Not the dramatic failure of our entire expedition, but the simple failure of low clouds, poor visibility, and the improbability of airplane flight. It was 9 a.m. on September 15. I looked out the window of the Alsek Air office, through wet gray air, across wet gray gravel, to the parked white and blue Cessna. Les, the pilot, had given us a 30 percent chance of making it to the landing strip at the Samovar Hills, where the ceiling would likely be even lower than in town.

Maybe one more day under a roof wouldn't be so bad.

Ready or not, we'd left the to-do list behind and made our way to the village of Yakutat along with 390 pounds of food, 427 diaper pads, and 62 pounds of gear. Some of it had traveled with us on the twice-daily jet, cinched into lumpy blue nylon sacks, luggage tags taped to the outside. Some of it had come by mail, set aside in a great pile of heavy duct-taped boxes by the friendly postmistress (who'd also fed us dinner).

Yakutat felt familiar. Homey. Four years earlier, its school was the first we'd ever visited as official presenters. Yesterday we'd returned, flashing pictures and maps on the screen, while the kids giggled and laughed at the image of their younger selves. They remembered their birthday present to Hig that day: a two-pound block of cheese. I kept circling back to those stories, their words forming a solidly real contrast to the wispy hopes and plans of the journey we were about to begin. I didn't want another day of electric lights and electric anticipation. I wanted this all to turn real.

We took our 30 percent chance, watching the beaches streak past below us and willing the clouds to rise. And then they did. I glued my face to the window as the plane flew over the sinuous curves of brown and white ice, talking to Hig in excited crackling bursts over the airplane headphones. You can never really tell anything from the air. But still, our plan looked possible! It looked amazing.

The plane ground to a halt amid the willows and lupines of a gravel bar landing strip, disgorged us with all of our gear, and quickly took off again. Feet planted in the Samovar Hills, I watched the plane disappear in the direction of Yakutat and realized that the countdown was finally over. We had all the time in the world.

MALASPINA
GLACIER

N ←

10 miles

• Camp
⌇ Trek route
- - - Edge of glacier ice

MALASPINA
GLACIER

Malaspina Lake

Samovar
Hills

Sitkagi Lagoon

Fountain
Stream

Bare ice

Gravel-covered ice

Vegetated ice

PACIFIC
OCEAN

PART IV

Life on Ice

13: Visiting the Ice Age

A STEADY DRIZZLE followed us to the head of the valley, where steep talus hills butted up against a ridge of crenellated peaks, rising abruptly from the valley floor. Where we walked, stream channels braided across an expanse of gravel, the higher spots marked by almond-shaped patches of lupine and willow. Here it was raining, but the sheer face of rock above us was striped white with the dusting of last night's snow. Above that face, more snow and more mountains, the eighteen thousand feet of Mount Saint Elias standing infinitely higher and vaster, only fifteen miles away yet barely visible from the depths of our valley.

Katmai whined about his cold hands. *That's what happens when you plunge your nice dry mittens into an icy stream immediately after we put them on you!* But instead of shouting out the I-told-you-so, I muttered it to myself, out of toddler earshot. I knew that level of common sense was beyond a two-and-a-half-year-old's brain. I knew he was tired. I knew it was simply a collision of immature moods and an imperfect world. Hig swung Katmai up onto his back, arranging him in the wrap with his hands tucked against dad's warm neck.

Whining was easy here. Not just for the kids, but for me as well: *The kids aren't letting me get anything done. The kids are screaming at me. Lituya is*

Erin walks among stranded icebergs at the edge of the Samovar Hills.

fussy. My feet are cold. It's awkward to wear Lituya on front. I don't like crossing this opaque glacial water carrying the kids. I wish we had a drier place for the baby to play. I wish Katmai would fall asleep more quickly. I wish. . . . Two days in, the kinks in our system were as numerous as the solutions.

But already the days were strangely, wonderfully relaxing.

A sharp whistle rang out from the rocks ahead of us.

"Marmot!"

"No, it must be a bird."

The whistles kept coming, long and shrill, and utterly marmotlike. Marmots are fuzzy rodents that resemble guinea pigs and live in alpine boulder piles. It wasn't strange to see them in Alaska, but it was strange to see them *here.*

The Samovar Hills are an island of tundra ridges and brushy slopes, cut by gravel river valleys—twelve miles long by three miles wide. And they are ice-locked. It's two and a half miles to the nearest nunataks—isolated peaks of rock piercing the ice. It's five miles to the nearest similar set of hills. Fifteen to the forested ocean coast, where we were eventually headed. In our planning, I imagined this island as a barren outpost, populated only by life arrived on wind or wing. We'd looked, and failed to find, any sign of voles or other tiny mammals. But there were bears, perhaps loping across those fifteen miles in a single day. And now the marmots—leaping crevasses on their stubby legs? There were even finger-length fish in these isolated streams—defying all my attempts at explanation. The drizzle beaded up on our brand-new coats, leaving only the breath of a chill. We scrambled through steep boulders on the river's edge, its roar making conversation impossible, sending us both into our own silent thoughts.

Back in the flats, Hig came up to walk beside me, hugging a daypack stuffed with clothes and food. Katmai's sleeping head lolled back from his shoulder. "I've been imagining what it would be like to be the first person to paddle to the Samovar Hills."

I'd been imagining how we should approach if there's a bear standing in our tent.

Both of our minds had wandered to detailed and unlikely scenarios, in our characteristically different ways. To ward off the bears, we'd spent an hour carefully stringing up the electric fence around the perimeter of our camp, then promptly forgotten to turn it on. My imaginary disaster was close up and personal. Hig's imaginary disaster was beyond our own lifetimes. I thought so, anyway. But Hig the geologist insists it might not be. A century? Or just a few decades? Until the end of the glacier's own lifetime, when the rapid melting set off by climate change will turn the lobe of ice into a lobe of ocean, and our alpine valley will hang perched above the waves of a brand-new fjord.

The end point of this journey would be around a hundred miles from its beginning—a hundred miles of moving every piece of gear that we owned. But on many days, we made no progress at all toward that eventual sum. Instead, we left nearly everything behind the ticking electricity of our bear fence. Instead, we climbed.

"No, you cannot push your sister over. Sure, you can have some raisins. They're over there next to your animals. No, she's not even touching your animals."

Hig refereed from the other side. "No, Lituya, you can't crawl into the fire. I know, it looks like so much fun. Here, you can play with this pot lid, or these socks."

"Lituya," I added, "boots are not for eating. Cords are not for eating either. Katmai, you're too close to the stove."

"Hey, Erin, what am I supposed to be packing in this one?"

"Food. It's in a pile on the red dry bag."

After coffee and oatmeal and clothing and diapers and hanging a day's worth of gear across our bodies with an assortment of pouches and straps, we climbed. We climbed as much as our out-of-shape bodies and the patience of the kids on our backs would allow. Ptarmigan erupted from the bushes with startled croaks. Hawks wheeled circles above the ice.

The ice. This was the view I had been waiting a year to see. Squinting into the sun across the vast lobe of Malaspina Glacier, the ocean of ice was as impressive as I had ever imagined. It began in sinuous stripes of gray and white, where gravel moraines curled across the plain of ice, disappearing to a blue ocean smudge at its farthest edge. To the left, my eyes followed puzzle-piece crevasses to the next set of mountains, where the ice bulged to engulf them as well, stretching toward the distant water of Yakutat Bay. To the right, the Samovar Hills dropped into a lake of jumbled icebergs, blending into a jumble of crevasses, to another island of ice-locked peaks, and yet another glacier-fringed bay.

It was as vast as I could have imagined—a frozen ocean with hills of gravel sticking out like islands in the sea. It was like nothing I had ever seen in the world.

"There are holes for marmots to go in, and I have a pretend marmot and—THERE ARE BERRIES!" Excitement raised Katmai's already shrill voice up an ear-splitting octave. Interrupted in my reverie, I turned my attention to where he had belly flopped into a patch of alpine blueberries, eating them as fast as he could pick. The vastness of the glacier, the height of the peaks, the sheer otherworldliness of an ice-locked land. All of that skipped over Katmai entirely. Lituya sat on the tundra beside him, screeching at the temptation of berries and the clumsiness of eight-month-old fingers. Where my world was mountains, the kids' world was pebbles.

⌒〇⌒

A few days later, we traced the edge of that ice, between Malaspina and the Samovar Hills. Waterfalls poured from dark holes in cliffs of glistening ice. Streaks of muddy water spattered down the hills. We walked the barren canyon in between, where creeks slunk under icy overhangs, fissures appeared in piles of gravel, and streams burbled into nothingness.

It made me think of home. This chunk of lumpy hills could be the ridge behind our house, where minor advances of a mostly shrinking glacier pushed up a series of mini-moraines, rumpling the surface. That network of ice-edge streams might be the branching gullies on either side of our driveway. The stream flowing through that notch might be the depression in front of our friend Chris's house, where a glacier blocked the obvious path for water—forcing a river to cut through a hill beside it. This was our home as it might have looked ten thousand years ago, when Kachemak Bay was filled by Kachemak Glacier, leaving jumbled moraines in its wake as it retreated back from what would eventually become Seldovia.

We were visiting the ice age—walking on the ghosts of climate past. Malaspina is the only piedmont glacier left outside the Arctic—where mountain-born ice spreads out across a low-lying plain. And the Samovar Hills are one of the only remaining ice-locked landscapes larger than a solitary nunatak. All I had seen here was the exotic, a world so strange and unique that it resembled nothing else in our thousands of miles of wanderings. Once, such a world had been utterly normal. At the end of the last ice age, much of the continent was covered by glaciers or slowly melting out from beneath them. Enormous lobes of ice, just like Malaspina, filled most of Alaska's bays, valleys, and lakes. Nearly everywhere I've lived (Seattle, New York, Minnesota, Alaska) and most of where I've hiked was once beneath the ice. Malaspina is the last of a dying breed.

We could watch the transformation in bathtub-ring stripes, contouring the hillsides where ice-edge lakes once rested. In the record of time radiating out from the edge of the glacier—first mud, then colonizer plants, scrubby brush, and finally forest.

A shrinking glacier isn't remarkable. Glaciers are rarely at equilibrium, each one shifting with the particular details of its own microclimate. It's quite possible that over the ten thousand years since the last ice age, Malaspina has shrunk to something much smaller than it is today, and advanced to something much larger—perhaps many times over.

The remarkable thing about now is that it's nearly universal. No longer is each individual glacier following its own rhythm of advance and retreat based on local patterns of sun and snow. Nearly all the glaciers in the world are shrinking to the same beat, the details of place swamped by the overwhelming signal of global climate change.

We walked up and down the valley so many times that trails of our own rain-washed footprints nearly wiped out the signs of the bears that had come before. We walked everywhere within the five mile radius that would let us reach camp before dark—at kid-toting speed. We ate some of the hundred-plus pounds of food we started with, making our loads at least theoretically more manageable. And on the eighth day, we moved.

Hig had stolen scraps of time from our mornings, evenings, and rainstorms to build a contraption of bent green willows, our packraft (folded into a pinched seatlike form), the bicycle wheel, and a generous amount of string. A few hundred yards behind me, I watched him bend down, adjust one of the many knots, strap himself into the backpack lashed to the willow handles, then struggle to stand up under the load. My backpack rode in the raft beside all the things that wouldn't fit anywhere else, while the solar panel and ice axe were lashed to the raft's outer surface.

Katmai ran ahead, through fuzzy wet lupines sparkling in the sun, then stopped with a sudden grimace.

"Mom! I need to poop!"

"Okay, um . . . Let me . . . Wait." I definitely smelled something. "Did you already poop?"

"Yeah."

Our idea of continuing the potty-training effort on the glacier—of leaving a diaperless kid today in one of his only two sets of clothing— suddenly seemed much less clever. I had the kids, but Hig had taken all the stuff (clothes, cleaning supplies, everything) because Katmai was going to ride on my back, but then he decided to walk, and now . . . I grabbed Katmai's hand, more brusque than I needed to be.

"Come on. *Now*. We have to get back to Daddy to get something to clean you up with."

"Don't walk too fast, Mama!" he yelled, arm stretched out as he failed to keep my pace.

I switched from merely slow walking to glacially slow walking, trying to express a patience I didn't feel. At the base of the slope, something dark and furry moved. My heart jumped. No. Too small to be a bear. Its glossy fur was nearly black, with brown markings on its face and the edges of its flanks, which swept back to a broad flat tail. A wolverine! Extra clothes forgotten, I now wished I was carrying the camera. Only a dozen yards away, the animal hadn't yet noticed us but was staring intently at Hig and his packraft cart contraption.

In all our years in the wilderness, I've only seen a handful of wolverines, and never one so close. I stayed silent at first, noticing the twitch of his tail, the gleam of his fur. I couldn't bear to break the spell—until Katmai's chatter broke it for me. He watched the wolverine. I watched him watching the wolverine. The wolverine watched us. Then it bounded up the slope as a streak of black fur between leaves, pausing behind an alder to give us one last curious look.

In the background, I could still pick out the campsite we'd been struggling all day to leave, just half a mile behind us: 0.5 miles down and 99.5 miles to go. Didn't there used to be whole cultures that moved as families, across hundreds of miles? *But how?*

I woke to Lituya's kicks and gurgles, fumbling for the diaper bag in a new arrangement of gear. We had finally managed to move camp. Twice. Laboriously. Using all our best motivational speeches: "Oh look, I found a Katmai running trail!" "Walk to the next stick, and you can have another pineapple!" "Can you follow the tracks of Dada's wheel?" "Do you want to hold my hand or walk yourself?" "No, crawling isn't fast enough." "I'm going to count to three." "Now." And when motivation failed, we used the sheer power of muscle to carry them both.

Our gear was arranged in a pair of careful rings around our own bed (that we shared with Lituya) and Katmai's, with dry bags and backpacks plugging every conceivable sleep-scooting escape route. Piles of stones completed the barricade, preventing us from sinking into the floor. Our feet were earthquakes, turning the glacial silt we were camped on to Jell-O, then to a soupy foot-sucking goo. We'd placed stones strategically, paths to reach the stove and the door without becoming completely mired. But we slept. We woke. We could sleep here again. I was even willing to call this camp successful.

"Pass me the coffee?"

"Here, take the camera too. I think the sun's about to rise."

Balancing on the stepping-stones, with Lituya secured on my back, I ducked through our door into the world. I climbed past the tent sugar-dusted with frost, to the crest of a small rocky hill, pinching a camera battery in the warmth of my armpit, to urge a little more juice from the cold plastic brick. Sunlit mist touched down on the tips of the tallest icebergs. Yellow rays hit the toes of my not-quite-frozen shoes. Frosted rocks gleamed, and then started to melt, their slick wet edges blending into feathery crystals where sun met shadow. Hig joined me for a turn with the camera. Katmai threw rocks to break iced-over puddles, shattering concentric patterns in the ice.

This camp was fortified by a maze of icebergs, abandoned as their lake drained out under the ice. They were laced with cracks and bent with improbable overhangs, like hulking trolls, or turreted castles, or ravens and fish and all the animals Katmai could imagine. Ice glowed blue in the crevices, sun-cupped and wet. We ducked through tunnels and wound through paths between them. From the smaller bergs, I paused to chip us snacks of ancient ice.

Then we ranged too far. Many hours later, we returned through the maze in the dark, the bergs' gray shapes a looming confusion. Lituya wiggled in a fragile doze, calmed by my barely audible singing of "Twinkle Twinkle Little Star." Katmai slept deeply on Hig's back. We picked out Cassiopeia and the Big Dipper as the sky outshone the land, slowing our steps to be as smooth as possible in the stumbling darkness. Trying not to wake the sleeping kids.

"Are you sure this is the right way?"

"I think it's not too far now."

"Wow. I was so busy taking pictures this morning, I don't remember anything."

I didn't see the tent until we were almost on top of it. We followed our stepping-stones, avoiding the slowly freezing goo. Dinner was quiet that night, just the sounds of two adults slurping noodles and two limp bodies breathing softly in their sleeping bag cocoons. Our visions of difficulty faded into the calm of the evening.

❧

We had spent the day failing to reoccupy the site of one of Israel Russell's old photos, complete with Hig's sketchy scramble to scale the not-quite-right ridge while I waited with the children, the delay ensuring our failure to reach camp before dark. We had spent the day exploring a sharp-edged world of ice and gravel, weaving around crevasses, our footsteps crunching on crystals the size of Katmai's fist. We had spent the day destroying the battery charger for our camera, frying a hole right through the charger's plastic case—the first time our portable solar panel had seen the full light of the sun.

We discovered that problem the next morning. I looked around me at the dripping castles of ice, thinking of the photos I'd like to take, contemplating the heavy chunk of plastic and glass around my neck that had suddenly become a paperweight. I love photography. Oh well.

On an expedition, my natural tendencies toward regret are quickly pushed aside in favor of a stripped-down pragmatism. Things were always going wrong. And any problems that didn't look likely to be fatal weren't worth too much agonizing. We could try to hotwire something from one of our other chargers. We could see if the pilot could drop a spare out of his plane sometime in the next several days, since we'd left a spare in Yakutat. We could wait another few weeks until a visitor planned to meet us on the coast.

❧

The wonders of the Samovar Hills were jumbled up with hardship and frustration in a complicated mess, with the priority of each shifting moment by moment, tantrum by tantrum, and rain squall by rain squall.

In one moment, Lituya cries and tries to fling herself forward out of the wrap on my chest and Katmai arches backward out of the wrap on my back with his own whining scream. In another moment, Lituya is peacefully asleep and I listen to Katmai's long and inscrutable fable about a ptarmigan that died and turned into blueberries that the seed birds came and ate, pulling off their feathers and beaks and bones before blowing them into the wind. In one moment, I lean against the wind in a torrential rain, hurrying across the barren plain of gravel in a vain search for some less-damp sticks of firewood, wondering if the storm will ever end. In another moment, I sit on a ridge top with a view of the vast expanse of ice, surrounded by a carpet of nagoonberries—the most delicious berries in the world.

A wilderness adventure is a bipolar experience, marked by higher highs and lower lows than the vast majority of everyday existence. Living with small children is much the same. Combining the two—diaper blowouts and driving rain with perfect mountain vistas and childhood milestones—was having an amplifying effect on both ends of the spectrum.

14: Crossing the Moon

WE LEFT THE WHISTLING marmots behind. The wolverines. Fish.
Berries. Fields of lupine and the rain-filled craters left by bears digging for
their roots. Finally even the last of the alder bushes were behind us. The
last ptarmigan droppings. The last moss. And then one last pile of bear scat,
far out on a barren moraine. The rainbow of the living world had shrunk
to black, gray, and white, pocked with holes of radiant turquoise. We had
entered the ice.

It began with Hig in the tent, stuffing a dry bag to the brim with eight-
inch-long sticks, sawed from the dead branches of the last clump of alders
we found. With me, gathering every object we owned from its improbable resting place—scattered by the storm's whirlwind of tent-bound kids.
Sleet fell on our roof with a distinctive heavy hiss, coating moss and rocks
in patchy white. Miles behind and a few hundred feet above us, there was
nothing but snow. It buried the burrows of marmots and the berries Katmai
had searched out with such enthusiasm. The inexorable march of autumn
was chasing us down to the sea.

It began with one foot in front of the other, wedging my paper-thin
shoe into crevices between moraine cobbles while Lituya napped on my

The tent pitched on the ice of Malaspina Glacier, Mount Saint Elias
in the background

chest. The shoe was only a sheath of fluorescent green mesh, nearly transparent to the blades of rock and chill of ice. It was designed for "barefoot running," and I imagined a young, shorts-clad woman speeding over a mountain trail, unburdened by tents or babies. I loved the agile, slipper-like feel of the shoes, which added a tiny bit of grace to a system otherwise totally lacking it. But they weren't built for a hundred miles of broken rock, and by the end of the trip, patches of Hig's careful weaving nearly engulfed the muddy and faded fabric. In a similar pair of shoes, Hig was manhandling the packraft-bike wheel cart over the lumpy and shifting rocks, searching for smoother ground. My shoulders groaned just a little under the weight of the pack, which I knew would turn into a resounding complaint in a few hours. Neither the shoes, the raft, nor the packs were meant for what we were putting them through. Nothing ever was.

It was just another camp move.

But it didn't feel like just another camp move. This was the beginning of a Crossing. A slow-motion traverse of water long frozen into solid waves. Twenty-five miles from shore to shore that would take us a week to complete. As strange, unknown, and unnerving as any crossing of a river or bay. There would be no trees to shelter us from the storms, no brush to gather firewood, and no surface more than a rock's breadth from its chill. As we left the glacier's vegetated edge, we weren't sure when we would next see a living creature beyond our own small family.

In one photo, Katmai squats on a boulder in an orange fleece hoodie, bright red diaper, and homemade black neoprene boots, while Lituya stands propped up behind him, in her turquoise hoodie, orange diaper, and tiny wool socks. Mount Saint Elias looms before them in classic mountain perfection. But the kids don't see it. Katmai is looking down at the pebbles he has imagined into boats, and Lituya looks at him, wishing she could join in the game. Their backdrop is rubble—sharp-edged and barren.

"This is a rock boat, and it's swimming swimming swimming. . . . Off the edge!"

"Meh maaa gah?"

"Hey, Katmai, could you please climb back on that rock? We need you to be facing that way."

"Guuh, gahh, mah BAH!"

"I'll go move Lituya into the frame . . . " I told Hig. "Wait. I think I need to change her diaper again first."

"Okay, I'll switch lenses."

Their play was perfectly genuine. But everything else was staged—an attempt to get some kind of photo for our diaper company sponsors.

Through the miracle of satellite phone technology, we had managed to finagle an air-drop of batteries and charger from our stash in Yakutat, bringing the camera back to life. Every evening, I used the phone's awkward keypad to type in updates, sending them to a friend's email in 160-character bursts. When the movie from our four-thousand-mile journey showed in film festivals around the world, we got calls on that phone, answering questions about being cold and wet in the Alaskan wilderness while pacing in front of the tent in the cold and wet Alaskan wilderness. Until the signal inevitably cut out.

I put the kids' pants back on. Hig fiddled with the packraft cart, adjusting the solar panel draped on its southwestern flank, carefully securing three sets of fiddly connections against the jarring ride over boulders. "Should we charge the other camera battery?"

"No, I think the sat phone first."

Every moment the sun appeared, there was some piece of technology we needed to try to charge. A few years ago, we didn't carry half of this equipment. Our photo and film goals were less ambitious. Communication wasn't an option. We said goodbye when we left town and hello again when we reached the next one. Now we *could* communicate. So now we wanted to. Now we almost felt like we *had* to. It was complicated and distracting. It made more things possible. It made more things expected.

My favorite photo is from a little later that evening. On my chest, Lituya is no more than a sleeping lump, visible only as a red triangle bulging from my half-unzipped coat. My pack is taller than I am, with dry bags sticking jauntily out the top, and a blackened pot dangling from one side.

Katmai clutches my hand as we walk over cobbles, wearing three layers of fleece against the chill September evening. Behind us again is Saint Elias, bursting out beyond the frame.

Hig disappeared ahead of us. First to take the photo, then off with the tent, making camp another three-quarters of a mile away, adding to the two miles we'd already traveled. My grasp steadied Katmai's small legs against loose rocks and patches of black ice.

"Is that an elephant up on that hill!!?" I asked in my best pretend voice.

"Oh yeah! I see it! And I see a *giraffe*! See, it has a long neck, *right there!*"

We picked out boulders silhouetted against the setting sun, naming them as houses, elephants, and whales—each hundred yards a new and exciting destination. Katmai climbed them, swimming pebble boats in the puddles on their uneven tops, then leaping off into my arms.

"I want to jump again! Just two more times! Stand farther!"

He climbed dirt mountains, then lay on his belly to lap a trickle of water running over the ice. He chucked rocks into deep holes where imaginary creatures lived, crawled across the landscape like a snake, and rode on the backs of a boulder menagerie.

The sun left us in blue-gray shadow, and eventually Hig circled back, carrying Katmai the last quarter mile to where the tent perched on the side of a ridge, listening to Katmai's litany of "animal sightings." In the dimming light, the dark green of the tent nearly blended into the gray of the rocks, hills, and dips of shattered boulders stretching in all directions. I whaled at the ground with an ice axe, flinging chips of ice-encased gravel, hacking a flat spot beneath its roof just wide enough for four sleeping bodies. We retreated into the shelter, becoming caterpillars in our sleeping bags, using a ration of wood to cook a pot of oats—the fastest-cooking food we carried. Through the door, there was nothing to see but the vastness.

$\backsim$

I missed hot coffee. We had traveled with an in-tent woodstove for exactly two weeks of our adventuring life, and already I was spoiled. I measured the weight of the firewood bag in my hands, trying to translate a pile of sawed-off sticks to a measurement of warmth. "How many fires do you think we have left here?"

"Well, it depends what we're cooking, but . . . " Hig took the bag, his calculation no more than a brief glance. He would guess for me. Hig has been fascinated by firewood gathering, fire-starting, and fire-building from sometime around Katmai's age, and he's long since come to embrace those duties on all of our journeys. But that's not why he would guess. He would guess because confident and specific pronouncements—about how a task would be eighteen minutes, a route three and a half days, a project $450—is how he approaches the world. I envy his ability to brush aside uncertainty, even as I gripe about all the times the numbers, the route decisions, and the weather assessments are wrong.

He told me three. Three fires. Carefully rationed over the ice and rock, our wood was probably enough for three more hot meals. But not enough for this morning. Not if we wanted to eat hot food tonight. And never enough to make the whole tent warm. I wondered if the addiction of creature comforts was an inevitable downward spiral, where soon we'd find ourselves with camp chairs and extra shoes, thicker mattresses and bug-screened tents, until the load became so crushing that the adventures shrunk to a few miles from a road, but we didn't mind because all that suffering and striving ambition had worked itself out with youth, like college parties and all-nighters in the basement of the college biology lab.

But suffering was an overstatement. That was just the lack of coffee talking.

I snuggled both kids close, lingering in bed to delay the moment of eruption into icy air, savoring the measure of calm before the hurry to get everything and everyone ready as quickly as possible as my fingers chilled painfully at the touch of icy buckles and drawstrings and a frost-covered tent. We hurried to reach the only reliable place to get and stay warm—the secret that has always served us better than any fires or clothing or sleeping bags. Walking briskly. The pumping heart of a warm-blooded human.

"How are you doing, Katmai?"

"Good."

It was a grudging "Good," spoken just as the crying gulps had faded from his voice. He was tucked into the cart now, ensconced in all of our sleeping bags, only his eyes peeking from the pile of puffy insulation. At least I knew he wasn't cold. He probably missed the morning fire as well but hadn't yet mastered the art of sarcastic grown-up grumbling.

Snow fell. Thick and hard, coating the rocks in white and cutting our visibility to nearly nothing. Now the glacier, already mind-bogglingly massive, truly seemed infinite. There was nothing to see but an endless ribbon of ice, bounded by hills of rock-covered ice, slowly turning white with the snow. My feet were faster than the cart. Looking back, the fifty yards between me and Hig yawned wide in the swirling flakes, which also muffled the high-pitched squeals of Katmai's latest tantrum. They were stopped again. I was frustrated at yet another pause in our forward momentum, after all the other cart-fixing, crevasse-negotiating, and Katmai-placating stops this morning. But who could blame him? It was hard enough for me to step away from the immediacy of wet and cold to appreciate the stark poetry of our surroundings. How could I expect a toddler to do it?

From here, they were beautiful. A newly quiet Katmai, hidden within the raft, and a dad bent over him, fixing bumps in wild emotions with a judicious supply of dried pineapples. Feathery snowflakes sprinkled Hig's fleece hat and slid off the slick surface of the raft. The first snow of the fall is always beautiful. And as fleeting as the mood of a child.

A few hours later, the sun appeared as a moonlike disc behind the clouds, just enough to melt the snow piles into a wet slick on the surface of the rocks, before the night's freeze made everything solid again. Lituya woke up, gurgling happily. Katmai woke up, clambering out of the cart to walk on his own. Through my two layers of gloves and rain mitts, I gripped the soft bulk of his forearm, where his hands were tucked in to four layers of fleece.

"But I want to look down into the moulin!" he cried with excitement, tugging at my grip.

"Only holding Mom's hand," I replied firmly, tightening my grasp. I preferred his fascination with climbing boulders, but the hypnotizing

power of the moulins—vertical shafts where water poured into the
glacier—was hard to deny. We moved a few steps closer to the steep
rounded edge. A stream flowed snakelike across the ice beside us, wearing its channel smooth and gray-blue, until it poured over the edge in a
cascading waterfall, splashing and gurgling, the sound getting lower and
lower as the water spilled into the depths. The sides of the tunnel slid
from light blue-green to deep turquoise, inky blue, and finally to nothing.
I imagined the labyrinth of rushing tunnels and rivers that flowed beneath
the ice. Then I stepped back. Its depth pulled my eyes, as if the power of its
magnetism could sweep us straight off the flat ground we stood on, several
feet to the edge, into the darkness.

◦◦◦

The flap of slippery fabric in the wind and the constant drumming of
raindrops on nylon was the sound of coziness. The morning's dull light
penetrated the glacier all around the tent, reflecting up through our floor of
ice until it glowed a brilliant blue. I rolled over to grab a bag of half-stale
cookies, scattering crumbs on the bed as I ate.

"What do you think of staying here today?" Hig asked. "There are a ton
of places we could explore from right here, and . . . "

"The weather sucks? Yeah. I was thinking the same thing." When we
were a team of two we almost never stopped. In ten years, I could count just
a handful of times our tent spent more than one night on the same patch of
ground. Now, after moving camp several days in a row, I was already itching
to stay put. Or at least for the gear to stay put.

"I'll take the first walk? I think Lituya could use more sleep."

Rain or no rain, neither of us wanted to stay in the tent. I can learn
to be fascinated with a flower or a bug. In fact, we were all fascinated by a
whole world of mysterious black bugs an inch or two below us, crawling
through microscopic fractures in seemingly solid ice. But I have outgrown
the joys of vrooming a headlamp-turned-truck around a sleeping pad.

We took turns. Hig helped me arrange my double rain hood over
Lituya's head behind my back. The rain quieted as soon as I left the tent, no
longer drumming on the roof and muffled by the sound of the hood. Where

it crept into my sleeves and around the edges of my neck, it felt like nothing more than water.

It's a testament to the size and awkwardness of our usual loads that a twenty-pound baby felt featherlight. She slept with her head slumped into my shoulder, and I felt the slight pressure of each rise and fall of her chest. Throughout the journey, she slept much of the time I walked, lulled by what rhythm there was on the rough and uneven terrain. I wandered aimlessly, framing the world in a rain-spattered viewfinder. Water sheeted across the surface of the ice, neatly filling the holes and smoothing the pockmarked surface, until it was nearly impossible to tell if a footstep would land on a pillar of ice or in a knee-deep hole. Solid turned to liquid, and they both looked exactly the same.

∽

The next morning, I noticed that a full inch had melted away around us. Our tent had insulated the ice, and in just a day, the drizzle of rain had cut through everything else, washing it down into the moulins and out into the ocean beyond. If multiplied by nearly a thousand square miles of glacier, that shrinking inch adds up to tens of millions of cubic yards of ice. Multiplied again by days, months, or years, the number grew staggering. We were watching ice melt, intricate and beautiful in its details, terrifying in its multiplication.

This part of the glacier has always been melting. High in the mountains, more snow falls each winter than can melt in a summer, until the weight compresses it into a lobe of flowing ice, spilling down onto the plains below. In these lowlands, more snow melts than falls, to be replaced by new ice flowing down from above. When the two sides equal each other exactly, the glacier stays put. When snow overwhelms melt, the glacier starts to grow, bulldozing forests in its path. When melting wins, the glacier shrinks.

Melting is winning. Across its vast surface, Malaspina loses around five feet of ice each year. Less in the mountains. More where we were standing. This is the ice that raises the oceans. Together with its neighbor the Bering Glacier, Malaspina has been responsible for 0.8 percent of global sea level rise since the 1960s. A small-sounding number—disproportionately large. These glaciers are only 0.005 percent of the world's land. And they supply more than two cubic miles of brand-new seawater every year. Adding in the rest of the Gulf of Alaska, the melting death of glaciers spills out enough water each year to equal five Colorado Rivers. Statewide, Alaska's shrinking ice can claim credit for a third of the melt in the sea, nearly a tenth of the sea level rise that's already happened.

The ice that melted away around our tent is becoming the unstoppable torrent that will drown Kivalina, the Maldives, Bangladesh, Florida, and thousands of cities along the world's coasts. Not just two cubic miles of water a year, but more water each year as the melting accelerates.

I could hear the ice disappearing. In contrast to popular stereotype, the wilderness is almost never quiet. Wind whistles through the trees and rushes over open country. Rain patters on leaves. Birds screech, mosquitoes drone, streams burble, waves crash, and our footsteps swish and squelch and crunch over all the variety of terrain. The ice was different. Each morning, we woke to a landscape frozen as still as anywhere I've ever been, with only our own thin voices to break the air.

The silence was marred first by tiny popping sounds. Then faint hisses and musical tinkles, as the warmth of the day softened and broke a thousand fragile edges. We listened as ice turned to water, gurgling in ankle-deep streams, sluicing through snakelike channels, then cascading into moulins with a deep and infinite roar. Rocks melted loose from unseen purchases, punctuating the flow with occasional clattering tumbles. Katmai added his own loud splashes, as he rolled and pushed rocks into a desk-sized puddle, watching them disappear into the infinite depths below.

"Be careful!" I called.

"I'm walking very slowly and carefully so I don't fall in," he assured me, balancing on the rounded edge of ice.

"Be careful!" I admonished again, still hovering—my fear of that deep blue hole warring with my love of childhood exploration.

"The pool is full to the top," Hig pointed out with characteristic nonchalance. "It's not like a moulin—there's nowhere to fall. And you're right there watching him. All he could do is get wet."

At night, temperatures dropped, slowing the melting until it stopped altogether. The water drained into crevices and disappeared into the moulins, leaving our ice road dry, cold, and silent again.

～⌒～

For several days, we'd been following an ice road. I couldn't escape the analogy. It was as hard as pavement, as wide as a multilane highway, and actually divided into lanes by a center stripe of cobbles—improbably more roadlike than anything else we'd encountered. Strewn across its surface were precarious-looking boulders tipping from pedestals of ice. Every hundred yards, our path was buckled and torn by a narrow V-shaped crack. Edging the ice road, rocky ridges rose fifty feet into the air, their tops rippled like the crests of a wave.

They *were* the crests of a wave. The cracks, the ripples, all were formed by the ice flowing and buckling beneath us. The rock that defined them was almost an illusion, a single layer of insulation that protected the crests from the warm summer air that melted the valleys.

If the 840 square miles of Malaspina Glacier were an average piece of the country, it would be home to over seventy-four thousand people, with actual highways connecting shopping malls to neighborhoods of neatly painted houses. Even as an average piece of Alaska, it would be home to about a thousand. Here, there were exactly four people. Soon to be zero again.

Ice, rock, mountains, water, sky. In white, gray, and turquoise, those five ingredients arranged themselves into an infinity of forms, from the sweep of the glacier against the peaks of Saint Elias, to the intricate geometry of bubbles in the ice. Beautiful, fascinating, and barren. It felt as unearthly as when we'd first set foot on it, growing familiar but never quite comfortable.

～⌒～

The packraft–rickshaw cart had finally met its match, where each foot of distance gained through lifting, tugging, and pushing through the chaos of boulders was both painfully slow and just plain painful. Hig walked away from the splintered willows, bicycle wheel dangling from the outside of his pack.

"I feel like I've gained so much freedom."

Freedom, in this case, was the freedom to walk with a heavy pack on his back and a wiggling two-and-a-half-year-old on his chest, over a stretch of ice turning from white to gray-brown and lumpy with boulders, cobbles, and narrow crevasses. I mourned the loss of Katmai's favorite napping spot, felt grateful for the increase in speed, and wondered if the bizarre idea had been worth it at all.

I could catalog a whole list of gear maimed or dead at the hands of the glacier. All four of our shoes, hanging on by Hig's woven threads. Water bottles made bizarrely spicy by an accident with one of the canisters of pepper spray we carried as a bear attack deterrent. A camera charger's fraying connections, designed for a life in a gentle office. A tent zipper killed by the ever-present silt, and Katmai's rain suit zipper not too far behind.

We could see Fountain Stream reflecting in the distance, marking the edge of our crossing. Beyond, the yellow pyramids of cottonwood mingled with dark-green spruce. I coveted those trees. Or at least the warmth that burning them would create.

"It's 12:45 and we've gone three-quarters of a mile. But I think we'll do better later," Hig commented hopefully the next day, as we stood on a ridge looking out toward Fountain Stream, still impossibly far away. The area leading up to Fountain Stream is a maze of steep ice cliffs and between them, steep and unstable slopes of sharp-edged cobbles and boulders. Every single footstep required an exhausting precision, moving crablike to see around the protruding baby head on my chest, leaning on the ice axe as I picked my way along. One hand supporting her head, waiting impatiently for the moment she'd fall asleep so I could tuck her head in and gain a few precious inches of ground-viewing capability.

Hig followed behind, with Katmai in a similar position, his load even heavier than mine. "I don't know what you'd do if you did slip with a kid on front like this, to not clonk their head on a rock."

"Your arm could land first. At the expense of an injured arm most likely. That's why I just walk really slowly and carefully," I said, shrugging. Hig had been using the cart for transport for most of the past week, and the kid-plus-pack toting combo was newer to him than it was to me.

I squinted into the sun, uncomfortable in the unseasonably hot and sunny air, the pack and Lituya providing unwelcome insulation as well as their burden of weight. Just a few days past a stretch of unbroken cold, I knew it was an ungrateful complaint. Temperature is a feeling of the moment. In one instant I huddle in every scrap of clothing I own, wishing and wondering if I'll ever be warm again, sure I'll appreciate any glimpse of warmth with undying gratitude. Then I don't. With the first sweaty prickle of heat, the whole concept of cold melts away to an insubstantial memory. And the cycle repeats itself.

The kids had eyes only for the mud. Lituya crowed with delight at the glassy-smooth surface and took off in an asymmetric crawl, chasing her brother as he jiggled it with exuberant stomps, digging "holes for ants," and penning abstract renditions of S and K with an alder twig. I had eyes only for those alders, their dead branches forming a promise of melted cheese and steaming noodles.

Our crossing was complete. We had reached the realm of mud and plants—and ice. The glacier wasn't really behind us. It was still beneath us. But at this outer edge, silt-filled ice melted down into silt, glazing the glacier with a feet-thick frosting of soil. Forests grew on it. I felt a psychological boost that only being back in the land of the living could provide.

The *living.* There were wolverine tracks. Fresh. Moose tracks cratered the ground between willow bushes at every stop along the river's edge. And bear tracks. Near that first camp, there was only one fresh line of prints. The next day, we paddled to a tiny island where each claw on the tracks was so astoundingly clear that Hig circled the island with bear spray clutched tight—scouting every bush. Piles of scat littered the beaches. At our next landing, more of the same.

Maybe the land of the living didn't sound so good after all. I knew *living* meant bears. But listening to my tiny children squeak like marmots as they played on the beach, I almost longed to be back on barren ice—for infinite visibility and the reassuring notion that there was nothing there for a bear to eat.

"The bears aren't more of a risk just because we haven't seen any for a while," Hig pointed out. "We've traveled lots of places with a similar level of traffic, including the coast up ahead, and if anything, we're better prepared now."

I *did* believe bears were a small risk, and one that we were cautious of and well-prepared for. But I'd hoped for a longer reprieve. I was accustomed to bears, but maybe I'd never be fully accustomed to parenting-near-bears. Each expedition, they worried me more. Further down the river a small brown bear cruised the beach, dark and slick in the rain, and bolting as soon as he caught our scent. As Hig steered the raft, I floated backward, listening to the growing roar of the surf. From a gravel riverbank, we followed a bear trail through grass and brush, suddenly arriving on a shore of sand, cobbles, and more numerous bear tracks, accompanied by the foam-topped curls of endless strings of waves.

Watching the crashing surf, I felt like we'd completed a great migration—from ice-locked hills to the salt of the Pacific. It made me swell with a sense of accomplishment not matched by the middling ordinariness of the twenty-first day of a sixty-one-day expedition. I wondered if anything yet to come could possibly measure up.

15: Kids in the Woods

LITUYA'S EYES WERE CLOSED, tucked beneath the crook of my arm, nursing to sleep in the dark cocoon of the sleeping bag, in the dark cocoon of the tent. I closed my eyes as well, letting my mind fly along on Hig's accounting of the adventures of Ziggy the Raven. Alongside our very real adventures, a stable of anthropomorphized animals and fantastic creatures concocted their own wilder explorations of Malaspina Glacier, where seals swam through tunnels beneath the ice, ravens flew to the moon, a bear and a marmot became friends with the fearsome Malaspina Monster, a moose rebuilt an old sailboat, mountain trolls ate rocks, and swans went skiing down the slope of Mount Saint Elias.

At home, we would have read Katmai a story from a shelf overflowing with picture books. Here, the only words were on the pages of my journal, on the wrapper of a chocolate bar, and in our own imaginations. On this evening, Ziggy the Raven and his friend Mushi the Swan were surfing the curling waves of the Lost Coast on pieces of driftwood. Actual crashing surf provided a low-level background to the story, and in the distance a flesh-and-blood sea lion bellowed his guttural "Ourraaaaagh!" for a touch of authenticity. The nightly stories wound their way into our daily reality,

Lituya and Katmai play in the tent, their home for two months.

where Katmai spent his days chatting about the characters, seeing Ziggy in the trees, detailing the eating habits of different kinds of trolls, and making up his own tales of hole-digging, mountain-climbing eagles. I'd come to look forward to the stories nearly as much as he did, all the challenges of the real day behind us melting away into the fantastical world.

Food caches were like Christmas twice a month. But the joy of all those brand-new bags of pasta, nuts, and fruit was quickly drowned beneath the overwhelming weight of their forty brand-new pounds. Our tracks sunk in the sand. Hig tried to convince Katmai to walk because he just couldn't carry any more, until the boy was so tired that there was nothing to do but drape him upside-down on Hig's shoulders like a towel, napping with his face in the rain.

We wanted nothing more than to stop, and sleep. But we were picky. We needed a site we could get to easily from the beach. Protected from the wind. With water handy. And most difficult of all, not on a bear trail and unlikely to become one. We rejected the alder thicket. The marsh. The deep dark forest with no trace of fresh water. The moss as soft as a feathered pillow, speckled with wildflowers and laced with bear trails. Hig ran into the woods to scout each one while I sat heavily on the beach, sleeping Lituya still strapped to my chest, Katmai awake again and drawing pictures in wet sand.

Daylight's end found us a small damp patch of moss untrammeled by bear tracks, with just enough room to place the bed beyond the growing pool of water—or at least we hoped there was. Lituya cried her wordless exhaustion as we raced dark to set up. Through her screams, I reached into dry bags, pulling out sleeping bags and fleece suits. Katmai asked "Please could somebody snuggle me?" and "Where's my bed?" with heartbreaking politeness. Both kids fell asleep on top of me. Hig tied the last knots in downpour and darkness, the light from his headlamp flashing through the nylon walls.

Katmai was a real trooper. Which is what a parent is supposed to say when a small child suffers the strain and difficulty we have put him through with more grace than we can reasonably expect from a two-and-a-half-year-old. It's a shorter way of saying, "Thanks for not having a tantrum, even though most adults would have."

Kids are tough because they don't yet know they shouldn't be. Because they don't understand that being cold and tired in the middle of the wilderness is any worse than not getting a second piece of chocolate or the crushing disappointment when your sister knocks over your carefully constructed tower of blocks. A flash of strong emotion, in a swirl of circumstances you cannot control, in the clutches of people who will make sure you're okay in the end.

In the wilderness, we carry our home on our backs. For an adult, that is a practical truth—rain protection, cooking gear, and the insulation necessary to get a good night's sleep. For the kids, all the emotional depth of home was stuffed in a nylon bag, wrapped up in a bundle of green fabric. The tent was their small slice of security in a shifting and sometimes uncomfortable world. Until it was up at night, "home" simply didn't exist.

"See that brown thing out in the water?" I asked Katmai. "Do you see it? That's a sea lion!"

"Yeah." He peered listlessly out into the waves, but it was hard to tell if he really followed my enthusiastic pointing. I suspected he was just humoring me. For all the failings of our camp in a shady swamp, shedding dozens of pounds of gear and food beneath its roof sent me vaulting outside the next morning in an ecstasy of liberated lightness. With Lituya on my back, I nearly hopped from rock to rock, moving over the smoothed boulders with ten times the grace I'd felt the night before. Hig—with just Katmai, a camera, and a fanny pack of snacks—looked equally pleased. But the gleefully excited toddler face I'd been hoping for was simply a sleepy one.

The bellowing that had accompanied last night's storytime had faded away, and a few brown heads in the waves didn't match up to our hyped-up conversations. Four years earlier, and a month later in the season, Hig and I had stumbled on a sea lion haulout here. We hid behind a boulder to watch dozens of sea lions bellow their disagreements, young ones flopping on the blubbery bodies of their parents. Then we crashed through an alder thicket behind the beach, trying to keep a respectful distance as we made our way past them. Would they be here again?

I wanted Katmai to see them. Crossing the glacier, each day's mission was set by circumstance. We started at point A, and one way or another, we needed to get closer to point B. Today, we were free. I wanted Katmai to feel the joy of that freedom. We paused to play in the rocks at the top of the beach, watching foam crash over mother-baby pairs of sea lions as they swam just inside the break of the surf. Beyond them, others were scattered in ones and twos, jockeying for space on half-submerged rocks in a chorus of bellows and splashes.

They had swelled from brown specks into life-size animals now, and Katmai watched them swim by, a bit more interest sparking his eyes. He climbed the boulders, slowed a little by the slip of his rain suit on rock worn smooth by waves. We ate cookies. Changed diapers. And headed back the way we'd come.

"What's that thing walking?"

I kept my eyes on my footing, concentrating on the steps from boulder to boulder, answering offhandedly. "Dada?"

"No, that thing there!" Katmai insisted.

I looked up to see a massive sea lion a few dozen yards away, flopping into the sea.

"Ourraaaaagh!"

"A sea lion!" I cried back, startled by its sudden closeness.

"It's walking into the water! That's pretty funny! Do sea lions have feet?"

A moment later, it was gone beneath the waves. All the way back to camp and for the next several days, I listened to a monologue detailing that brief stroke of amazement, embellished by more and more elaborate tales of sea lion conversation, sea lion houses, and sea lion food.

Sea lions weren't all we had to reward Katmai with. As I thought about how our toddler got to watch sea lions and bears and wolverines and eagles, to throw rocks into glacial waterfalls, and to roam a scenic Alaska wilderness few adults have ever set foot in, it was easy to spin myself into a pleasant bubble of self-congratulation, the most awesome mother ever. On the other hand, he'd never realize a moulin was more special than a rock-lined puddle, or that a sea lion outranked a curious gull, or that he should appreciate the view of snowcapped peaks more than the face of an interesting climbing boulder.

Two-year-olds don't appreciate the extraordinary. They're too young to know normal—heedless of how their own experiences and opportunities might differ from others'. We can't explain that he's lucky to be here. Or that the blowing rain in his face and cold-finger mornings are just the price of existing in such an amazing place. He can't wonder why most other two-year-olds are on a soft couch watching TV instead of on wet boulders watching sea lions.

Katmai couldn't appreciate the extraordinary, because to him, everything—moss, sticks, icebergs, zippers—was extraordinary. And to him, it was all just life.

⌒⌒

I lifted the small metal circle from its hook and set the stove door down, sizzling on damp grass. A chunk of willow as thick as my wrist filled nearly all the space above the glowing coals. The firebox of the tiny stove was no larger than a gallon jug. It was the piece of our gear that did the most to stave off misery. But held to a diet of damp and scarce wood, it was finicky and demanding, needing almost constant attention. I had come to think of it as the third small child in our operation. Steam swirled in a bubble of stove-warmed air. Our bright red packraft stood fully inflated, taking up half the space in the tent, as if it were ready to paddle right out across our soggy meadow. With the kids.

"But I don't *like* splashes! Get her away from me!"

"Here, you can turn your back and scoot to the other end of the raft." Katmai was naked, swishing a tiny blue plastic shark back and forth in a quarter inch of lukewarm sludge. Lituya was also naked, both hands hitting the water with booming slaps, spraying gray silt over the both of them. Next to the stove, I sat by a cut-off buoy we'd scavenged from the beach, stirring the rest of the warm water into an appetizing soup of dirty cloth diaper covers, soiled clothes, and camp soap. It seemed likely I'd run through the stack of firewood Hig had left before anything really got clean.

"Maybe doing all these chores in an inefficient way is part of the beauty of being out here. Maybe it's kind of like extreme homesteading."

That was the thought Hig had left me with, while he hand-built a handle for his bow saw blade to saw our chunks of firewood. But he wasn't here now. He was walking east with a sat phone and a heavy bag of food, while I stayed home with two kids and a pile of dirty laundry. The "extreme diaper washing" hadn't yet won me over. I felt like I was a nomadic-hunter-gatherer wife, keeping the home fires burning while my husband went out for a big and bloody chunk of meat. Or I might have felt that way, with a little more competence.

If we were real hunter-gatherers, the ability to feed ourselves from the land would eliminate the need to deal with huge awkward bags full of ziplock-stored pasta and dried fruit, shipped halfway around the world and brought here by airplane. Hig wasn't even getting food, he was just leapfrogging some of our food ahead of us so we wouldn't have to carry so much across the boulders. If we were real hunter-gatherers, surely I'd be doing better at the simple task of bathing my family. Shouldn't I be the one doing all the firewood gathering and cooking as well as the child-minding? And sewing clothes, and gathering food, and constructing all the supplies for life without a wealth of high-tech plastic. How on earth would that even be possible? I'd never read a *National Geographic* article the same way again.

It hadn't gotten easier since last year. We'd gone from carrying twenty-one pounds of child to carrying forty-five. With two mouths, two bottoms, and two sets of exploring little fingers. Katmai's greater independence was more than canceled out by the constant demands of a baby just mobile enough to get into trouble and too clingy to put down. At only two and a half, he might have deserved more of my patience than he got. But it's easier to be charmed by a baby's guileless enthusiasm than by a toddler's articulated deviousness.

Hig cut firewood, stoked the stove, set up the tent, moved caches of food, paddled the raft, and strung up the bear fence. For my part, I pulled

Lituya away from the stove, held Katmai's hand as he climbed on boulders, policed sibling rivalry, changed diapers and clothes, prepared an endless assortment of snacks, and pulled an endless assortment of rocks from Lituya's mouth. The division of labor was practical, and with their ages, seemed inevitable. Hig's manly muscles were better equipped to move a heavy sack of food. My womanly bosom was better equipped to feed the baby. Despite our thoroughly nontypical existence, because of it even, we had fallen into the most traditional roles. Today I felt the loneliness of that tradition.

The tent is the kids' security object. But Hig is my security object, and I his. We had always relied on doubled hands, doubled legs, and doubled brains as an extra layer of safety—knowing that our own particular ways of evaluating the world combined into a unit more sensible and competent than either one of us alone. In an emergency, he had a satellite phone, and I had an emergency locator beacon. We each could reach the world. But we had no way to reach each other.

∽

It was the longest and least effective bath any of us had ever had. Time flowed around me in a formless blob, spiced by a mild backdrop of worry and wonder about Hig's slightly more glamorous mission. The tiny stove couldn't heat water nearly as fast as the air—in the forties—could cool it down. Katmai shivered, Lituya cried, and I snatched them out of the raft into the warm embrace of their least-dirty fleece coats, only to try again hopefully with the next potful. Their skin was baby smooth, startlingly pale, almost glowing beneath those many layers of fabric. Compared to our surroundings, they looked positively clean already. The month that separated us from running water suddenly didn't seem too long to wait.

Hours later, the diapers swung from a string in the tent's humid warmth. And we were finally outside it.

"Carry me!"

"I can't, I've got your sister on my back already. Come on, Katmai, I think you can get under this log right here. See, right by this branch."

"Oh yes, I *can* do that!"

We had gained only a few hard-earned feet when we ran into Hig, on the short but complicated path that separated our camp from the open beach. He lifted Katmai onto his shoulders and ducked through the final fringe of trees. Later, holding Dad's hand, Katmai ran through the sand at the edge of the waves, weaving through an obstacle course of giant boulders. Lituya sat nearby, stuffing fistfuls of sand in her mouth as if somehow the next one was sure to be more delicious than the last. I watched the tips of curling waves turn gold, as the sun slowly disappeared behind the surf.

I remembered the wall of logs. We hadn't built it—they were far too large for the two of us to move—but we had taken refuge behind it four years earlier, pitching our tent in the shelter of its lee. I remembered the huge column of flames against the dark night sky, when Hig added some choice pieces of beach trash to the driftwood pyre. I remembered our discussion through the sheeting rain, as I argued that the tent's shelter was the only way to stay warm and dry. From his perch by the fire, Hig countered that he could build a blaze large enough to keep up with the rain, his front side drying from the heat as quickly as his back could be soaked.

Arms outstretched, Katmai walked one of the logs as a balance beam. In four years, the evidence of our first passing had long since disappeared. And the transformation of a storm-battered camp into a sun-kissed toddler jungle gym stripped much of the drama from my recollections. Four years earlier, we'd stopped here on one dark and rainy November night, nine miles from the camp before, seventeen miles from the one to follow. Four years earlier, we'd been so inspired by Malaspina Glacier that we had to return. Four years earlier, we'd been lucky to see Malaspina Glacier at all.

Then, it had been a race against the food clock, and a race against winter, struggling to make it from the village of Yakutat to a food drop at Cape Yakataga, each of our days longer than November's brief daylight. Waking up in this spot, we'd chosen to go a few dozen yards inland to cross the silty stream. If not for that, we would have never have noticed the terraces of ice around the bubbling springs. We would never have noticed the glacier beneath our feet. Hidden beneath a plain of silt, thickets of brush, and the braiding of ankle-deep streams, the ice's presence was revealed only through the cold springs. Where super-cooled water rose from deep below the ground, freezing at the lower pressure of the surface, forming sheets and stairstep terraces of knobby ice that held fast to the streambeds.

The terraces are a few inches tall, obscured in most places by the silty water that flows over them. A super-cooled spring is not as dramatic-looking as it sounds. But it captured my imagination, on that first journey, because of what I couldn't see. On an unremarkable bit of coastline, we were actually standing *on a glacier*. On a glacier that extended hundreds of feet beneath our own feet, and hundreds of feet below sea level. What else was there that we couldn't see? That we didn't have time to notice?

⌒⌒

Crunch, rumble, sliiiiiiide . . . CRASH!

We followed the sound through a screen of brush, where the forest fell away into a silty brown lake. Literally. The forest grew on cliffs of melting ice, with three-foot diameter trees leaning precariously over the edge, and roots and trunks upended in the muddy water. We watched as head-sized boulders crashed on top of them.

Four years earlier, we hadn't seen this lake. Or the hillside forest we had come to call "Sleeping Beauty's Castle," where twisted trunks sprung from a carpet of foot-deep moss, sprinkled with rosettes of autumn-red dwarf dogwood leaves. Or the patch of hedgehog mushrooms, now piled into a ziplock for tonight's dinner.

We were spending a week in the few miles we'd once covered in a morning. Our progress was lumbering, inching—glacially slow. Compared to our pace four years earlier, we were barely moving. It was easy to feel less accomplished, to brush off the impact or achievement of a trip full of toddler-paced meandering. But a glacier is one of the most dynamic places in the world—if you take the time to watch it. At a few miles a day, feats of observation take over from feats of athleticism.

Back on the beach, Katmai climbed boulders, stepping carefully from rock to rock with steps that seemed outsized for his tiny body.

"You know, I'm envious of him, and of Lituya," I told Hig, "getting such an early start learning to walk in uneven terrain." I imagined them as ten-year-olds, vanishing ahead of me as they leaped between the boulders, far faster than I could ever hope to keep up. I looked forward to the day when I might become the straggler in the family.

But for now, they pulled back against our former pace, shifting us into a different relationship with the land. The craziness of Hig and Erin was no longer the only force shaping our adventures. Without the kids, we would never have struggled beneath such heavy loads. We would never have needed so many breaks to rest our shoulders, to nurse a baby, or to release the energy of a cooped-up toddler. Without the kids, we would never have planned a trip like this. It would have been faster and farther—an ambitious-looking line across a great swath of miles.

We would never have seen so much.

I knelt down with the video camera, ten yards away from Lituya.

"Come on! Come to Mama!" She looked at me, shuffled a foot or two in her asymmetric crawl, then looked sideways again.

Katmai burst into the frame. "I'm running and running and running!" He ran circles around us both, his bare feet spiraling tiny tracks in the damp silt, stealing Lituya's attention completely away from my attempt to entice her performance. My attempt to provide some evidence that she ever did something not strapped to my body. With her as the lighter (and still-nursing) child, and me as the less-muscular parent, we were natural partners. When she wasn't strapped to my chest, she was riding on my back, nursing on my lap, or playing at my feet. In the past month, she'd rarely been more than five feet away from me. But despite her constant physical presence, she only made fleeting appearances on the pages of my journal.

She was eight months old when we arrived on Malaspina Glacier. She'd be ten months by the time we left, spending a full fifth of her life on the journey. For me, the equivalent would be more than six years. This life might be all she could remember. Her whole world was me, her Dad, and her big brother—but mostly Mom. She'd only learned to crawl a month ago, and the sudden discovery that moving away from me was possible seemed to only make her cling tighter. Her crying would begin within seconds of a separation, followed by a desperate crawling dash in my last known direction. She crawled, but not well enough to cover much ground. She ate, but most of her calories still came from me.

But Lituya was there. She watched water rush into the moulins. She ate crowberries alongside Katmai on the ridges, struggling to manage her still-clumsy fingers. She mouthed rounded beach stones and fistfuls of gritty sand. She crawled, a fleecy mud ball leaving tiny handprints and drag marks behind her. She peered over my shoulder as we walked, her quiet gaze slowly turning to a singsong fussing, lowering in volume as she sung herself to sleep. Nestled tightly against my body, she slept through much of the country the rest of us saw. What does "here" look like to a brain so young? I liked to think of all those neural pathways being strengthened by the smell of salt air, the sound of wheeling seagulls, the vibrant blue of ice, and the feel of snow on her cheeks, rather than the flickering of screens and the smooth brightness of plastic toys.

Four years earlier when we passed through this spot, the kids existed not even in our imaginations. But Katmai was dreamed up in Icy Bay, thirty miles west, where we first decided to have a child. Lituya was named for Lituya Bay, 130 miles to the east. Bringing them both back here seemed to complete some kind of circle, an arcing story in my own head that had little to do with the kids themselves. They wouldn't remember this trip. Lituya was barely even aware of it as it was happening.

But in a few years they'd be old enough. And by then, Malaspina will have melted and buckled enough to be made new again, even for us. I hoped I could bring them back. The logistics were sure to be easier, but would they want to come? I blithely told most skeptics that of course all kids love to be outside. I figured that mine might grow up unaware that there were any other options.

Lituya might spend nearly every hour of her two-month "adventure" cuddled up with Mom. Because that's all a baby wants. The simple truth was that on an expedition, the kids got more of what they wanted than they ever would in "ordinary life." Not just more chocolate (although they did) or more wildlife sightings they would never remember. More of *us*. An expedition is a shared goal that can bring a family together. It had been true with just two of us. And it was now true for the four of us. Out here, the kids had both of their parents, every hour of every day, devoting far more of our attention to their explorations than we ever could at home. In a place engaging enough that we enjoyed it too.

⁓

A month into our journey, our first visitor arrived—a photographer from Anchorage whom we'd met online. Carl was on a multiyear mission to photograph all of Wrangell-St. Elias National Park. We had a mission to share our expedition with anyone who wanted to join us. Carl would travel with us for the next two weeks.

Katmai eyed Carl's proffered brownie with a heavy dose of skepticism. He accepted a piece reluctantly, but only from me and only after I ate some first. Chocolate itself, the source of who-knows-how-many hours of begging, had become suspected poison from someone else's hand. Lituya burst into screaming tears at the sight of another human, clawing her way onto my lap where she could nurse herself to sleep, as if his appearance was only a bad dream.

I might have hoped I was building nature lovers, but what I had at the moment was a pair of hermits.

16: On a Crumbling Edge

WE CALLED IT Dead Sea Lion Stream for the brown whiskered hulk lying at its mouth, still too fresh to stink. Water the color of a rainstorm sky poured onto the sand, waves rolling across its surface as it flowed into the ocean. It was the color of pulverized mountains. Of the glacier. Of everything around us.

We called it Dead Sea Lion Stream because it had no name on the map. Because it didn't exist on the map. The USGS had made their most recent map twenty-six years ago, in 1985, and since then the shrinking ice had resculpted the world so thoroughly as to turn its lines and curves into nearly useless decorations. Streams had appeared, dwindled, shifted miles along the coast, or combined into larger rivers. Ice-edge lakes had formed, grown, and disappeared. Beaches had eroded away. The dead sea lion was just a temporary landmark in a temporary world. But for us, it was paramount. In the course of two weeks, we would cross the stream four times, each time with a buildup of nervous anticipation, careful scouting, then a rush of relief when we found the corpse unmolested, no bloody-jawed bear standing guard over the prize. Only the footprints of ravens and eagles disturbed the sand.

Trees topple into the water of Sitkagi Lagoon, as the ice cliff melts away beneath them.

Traveling up the stream, a sudden ripple burst from the water, transforming into the wavering fin of a salmon. Then another one. The fish swam through a stream as clear as mud, into a lake equally opaque, headed for where? Silt chokes the oxygen from developing salmon eggs. And the glacier grinds down the mountains and valleys, turning everything to a fine muddy silt. On the four-year-old satellite photo we used for navigation, a few clear ponds appeared on the fringe of an upstream lake. The ponds were a few decades old, at most. These salmon, children of fish lost from some other stream, were the vanguard of a brand-new population.

The fish were here now. And along with them, a coal-black brown bear on the bank. He circled downwind, reared up on hind legs for a sniff, then disappeared into the bushes at a run, escaping a jumbled vision of a raft full of arms and legs and heads and the stench of unwashed human. The melting glacier brought whole new worlds for these animals to inhabit. Right here, this salmon and this bear were the winners of climate change, at least for the moment. But the ocean will reclaim this piece of land as soon as the ice leaves it behind. All across the ocean, climate change and acidification will shrink salmon habitat, deplete salmon food, and stress their eggs with the greater warmth of spawning streams. Perhaps halibut will live here next. Or maybe jellyfish.

~⌒~

Right now, what lived here was a sea lion. An inch-long plastic sea lion, diving beneath a pool the size of my hand. A similar plastic octopus traveled through a stream only slightly wider than itself, which I'd gouged into the silt with the point of a stick. Katmai leaned over the side of the deflated packraft, playing intently in the streams that ran around us.

"At least someone's happy about the flooded tent," I remarked.

"Hey, indoor pools are a feature!" Hig laughed.

Water sheeted across the silty ground, despite the trenches we'd cut all around the outside edges of the tent, and when those failed, around the inside edges as well. Hig's careful pyramid of firewood was slowly soaking through from the bottom up. Dry bags of food and clothes were abandoned to the puddles. All of us, the electronics, and all of the bedding were heaped in a pile on top of the packraft, constantly pulled back to center as wiggling children strove to scatter it into the flood. Inside, the stove roared. Outside, the wind did, spraying rain against our walls.

Glaciers grind the mountains to silt. We were on the edge of a glacier. We had been on the edge of a glacier for every part of the trip when we weren't actually *on* the glacier. So silt was what we got.

"I am never again camping on glacial silt." It was the third time I'd made this resolution in a month.

"It's actually a different problem this time," Hig pointed out earnestly, as if our discussions of permeability and sediment were merely a point of geologic interest. "The silt here isn't liquefying, but the water is running on top."

"It's the same cesspool camp either way."

"But the solution is different."

The only immediate solution was to move. When I first heard that Carl, our visitor, had brought two entire tents in his hulking backpack, I thought it was a ridiculous idea. Packing up my one-and-only tent in the center of a storm, it sounded positively genius.

The men scouted and set up the new camp. I packed up our gear in pools of water and in wind-whipped brush, picking up a screaming Lituya every time she crawled off the dry island of the sleeping pad I'd set her on. Katmai ignored it all, squatting happily in an ankle-deep pool to play with his "wood fish" until it was time to move. The eighth-mile trek to the new dry site (which was much easier to pick out now that all the other possibilities were underwater) felt as intrepid as a few minutes could be.

And then the world was dry, warm, cozy, playful, and okay again. The world was always okay again. That knowledge had carried me through countless windstorms, snowstorms, sleet storms, and long hungry trudges through the rainy darkness. But Lituya didn't know it yet. And my usual ironic jokes about whatever predicament we'd gotten ourselves into were harder to hear against her screams.

Around our new fire, the irony was perfectly audible—in my own voice and in Carl's Australian accent. Against the backdrop of Hig's persistently stoic optimism, Carl seemed to suffer in a style much closer to my own, cracking grumbling jokes about the stupidity of whatever had led us to the latest piece of unpleasantness. Like us, Carl had taught himself photography and how to travel in the Alaska wilderness—arriving, like us, at his own idiosyncratic style in both pursuits. After years of guiding novices through trail-less wilderness, he had the comfortable confidence that allowed him to crack those jokes. The same knowledge that we had. That everything, really, was okay.

◇◇

"Make sure you check for bears before you walk up onto that bank," I called out to Hig. "Maybe land the raft on the other side first, then . . . "

"Erin, I'll be careful. It'll be okay."

I watched Hig disappear though the door of the tent, packraft suspended over his shoulder on the end of the paddle, empty pack hanging loose from his back, weaving through the screen of willows between our new camp and the lake. Back down Dead Sea Lion Stream to pick up the next cache of food from where we'd left it hanging over a month ago. And hopefully to retrieve a missing canister of bear spray from where he'd lost it right next to the dead sea lion.

Sometimes it was a joke between the two of us. Sometimes it was utterly exasperating. And sometimes it was ammunition I used in my arguments against him. But it was incontrovertibly true: Hig loses gear. He breaks gear. He leaves it scattered behind him in places we may or may not ever be able to reach again. A small point-and-shoot camera, dropped on the rock-strewn ice near the Samovar Hills, and recovered half an hour later. A macro lens for our SLR camera, still sitting on a rock in the middle of the glacier—days behind us by the time we realized it. A knife broken splitting wood. A titanium fork broken prying coconut oil out of a ziplock bag. A battery charger dropped into a stream along with its complement of batteries, then melted in attempt to dry it out by the fire. I could continue the litany back to past expeditions, and I would be able to continue it forward through the rest of the trip—the catalog of possessions that had met their end with Hig.

But where I took care with the possessions we had, Hig had the creative energy to invent new ones and jury-rig repairs to the tattered remains of our own, replacing not only things he'd lost through carelessness but what we never had to begin with. He was the one who had woven the intricate patches of fishline that held together our fragile shoes. Built the packraft-cart in the Samovar Hills. Fixed all our zippers and wired together all our finicky battery chargers. But camera lenses and bear spray were beyond such solutions.

We had left the coast behind for this detour back to the ragged dirty edge of Malaspina. Rock on ice, interrupted on its lower flanks by an occasional patch of green moss, or an already leafless willow thicket. Interrupted by deep caves and ice tunnels, where tiny mud castles grew beneath the sound of a thousand drips.

"The edge is where everything is happening." That was the geologist's opinion. But I stumbled yet again on the uneven surface, stepping heavily, feeling yet another rock pierce my shoe. I strained to see my steps beneath the bulk of Lituya. I struggled to keep up with Hig and Carl, as tantalizing snippets of adult conversation drifted back in my direction. I leaned on a walking stick, which broke. I leaned on the ice axe, its metal tip ringing sharply against every rock. This route lacked the grandeur of the ice plain, the majesty of the coast's crashing surf, and the shelter and firewood of its forests.

I'd been telling Hig as much for the last several days. Carl agreed with me. And that was most of the problem.

Carl was an ideal guest. The three of us were experienced, comfortable in the wilderness, and got along well. Carl brought news from the outside world and opinions about current events. He pushed the adult-to-kid ratio high enough to dramatically raise the level of everyday discourse. But rather than adding a tie breaker, adding a third decision-making adult to the party complicated all our usual debates. Half the time, our world broke along gender lines. The guys scouted campsites and gathered firewood while I played with the kids. The guys scrambled over moraine boulders with a speed I couldn't possibly match, leaving me alone with the conversation of a nine-month-old.

The rest of the time it broke into enthusiastic ambition versus stodgy sensibleness. Hig pushed to stretch things. Each day hike a little farther, each camp move a little more ambitious. He operated on the principle that the least straightforward way would bring the most to explore. He had fallen in love with a route that would largely bypass the beaches of the coast in favor of this mazelike edge of geologic upheaval.

I was often in favor of inefficient plans. My whole life was an inefficient plan. But the constant travel on moraines was harder than I expected— on my shoes, my joints, and my morale. I argued not just for the slightly smoother rocks of the shore, but for the orange glow of sun on waves, the bellows of sea lions, and the shelter of trees. I was no longer the only Voice of Reason. With Carl and I in easy agreement, the balance was off—Hig felt we were ganging up on him.

We went to the ocean anyway, where another crop of visitors would tip the balance even further.

⌒⌒

Looking at the lemon, my mouth began to water. The kids were more direct in their begging. We all got some, savoring each morsel as the tart juice squirted out around the sharp and bitter peel. The carrot and parsley were equally euphoric. So much for self-sufficiency.

There were seven of us now. Our family of four, Carl, and now two more: Michael and Sam, building an increasingly gender-imbalanced team. The plane had disgorged them on a swath of sand just above the rising tide, a pile of overstuffed backpacks, shiny-clean gear, and extra bags beyond that for us and Carl, full of stuff we couldn't live without.

We had planned this journey to be self-sufficient. Not in a real living-off-the-land sense, but in a minor don't-need-to-visit-civilization-for-a-while way. We had every piece of gear on our spreadsheet and repair supplies besides. I had carefully counted out and weighed bag after bag full of not-too-perishable food, from noodles and oil to cheese, chocolate and fruit, then closed it all into odor-proof bags inside huge nylon sacks, separating two months of meals into a series of caches we could hang in the trees. The airplane that brought us out to the Samovar Hills should have been all that we needed until the plane that picked us up two months later.

Our plan failed immediately. First there was the cache the pilot had to hang for us because the tide was too high when we flew out. Then there was the camera charger fried by our solar panel, replaced via airplane. Once there was an airplane, we might as well get a few extra batteries and another toddler fleece. Carl came with another airplane, which we commandeered to lighten our packs of trash, the bicycle wheel that no longer seemed useful, broken gear, and assorted items of kid clothing that never worked out quite the way we intended.

Those were minor conveniences. But the plane that brought Sam and Michael was a crutch. Our first food cache (hung by the pilot) was in perfect condition. Our second one had not been so lucky. While we failed to divert the water sheeting beneath our floorless tent, the same storm whipped the branches of that coastal forest, plopping our food bag onto the equally flooded forest floor. An earlier storm had knocked down its twin. Abandoned in that swamp, water had been slowly leaking into our food for a day, or a week, or who knows how long, worming into the inevitable holes in ziplock bags and seeping through their slightly faulty seals. Most of it was recoverable. Some was not.

The self-sufficient option would be to go a little hungry—to walk faster to the next cache. We could have done it. But that airplane was coming. . . .

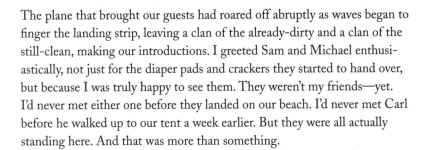

The plane that brought our guests had roared off abruptly as waves began to finger the landing strip, leaving a clan of the already-dirty and a clan of the still-clean, making our introductions. I greeted Sam and Michael enthusiastically, not just for the diaper pads and crackers they started to hand over, but because I was truly happy to see them. They weren't my friends—yet. I'd never met either one before they landed on our beach. I'd never met Carl before he walked up to our tent a week earlier. But they were all actually standing here. And that was more than something.

We'd planned this journey with a nearly open invitation. Anyone who could manage to get themselves out here—and was reasonably confident they could survive the journey—was welcome. Sam was a few years younger than Hig and me, a quiet and bearded Midwesterner with a propensity for abstract discussion and luxurious food. He was the source of lemon, parsley, and carrots, and could often be found lunching on hard-boiled eggs from a yellow plastic egg carton. He was a digital ghost made suddenly solid. He was a computer programmer we'd been working with remotely for years, someone whom I knew only from inscrutable emails full of jargon I didn't understand. Someone whom I reached out to solve obscure bugs in website administration and photo uploading. Untethered from that world, I didn't recognize Sam at all.

Michael was probably in his forties (we never asked), an enthusiastic professional weather forecaster, and an equally enthusiastic misadventurer. His conversation included a worryingly endless series of near-miss near-death stories in the woods, told with cheerful nonchalance, all the way up to being hit by lightning. We knew him also as a digital form—from a series of terse and abbreviated text messages we'd read on our sat phone, weather forecasts built just for us.

Our tent was the party tent, where everyone wedged onto sleeping pads around our tiny woodstove, five adults chatting by the light of five differ-ent headlamps. Lituya reached for the headlamps as irresistible toys, before finally crawling over to fall asleep in my lap. I split my attention between the talk of backpacking gear and ordinary lives, and Katmai's insistent and largely unrelated monologue: "P is for pony. T makes a *tuh-tuh* sound, like *teeth* and *tent* and *tie* and *tea*. And *iced tea*. I like iced tea. And I like mint tea. I like two kinds of tea. Do whales have eyelids? Do they have tongues? Do they have flipper floppers? What do whales like?"

⌒〜⌒

Squalls drummed on the rubbery surface of the raft as we paddled around the edge of the lagoon. Our family was wedged into a single red packraft, while Sam followed in his own blue boat a dozen yards behind us, and everyone else waited in the shelter of camp. Drops snuck down Lituya's face where she slept on my lap, made ripples in the gray water, and washed streaks of white down the dirty gray ice cliffs, like the staining of rocks in the desert.

We had brought them to Sitkagi. Sitkagi Bluffs on the map, Sitkagi Lagoon in current reality. This is the place where the mass of Malaspina meets the even larger force of the Pacific, where seawater crumbles its frozen cliffs, and ocean slowly triumphs over land. A small tidal stream, rocks painted green with a film of algae, connects the ocean and the ice. On a map that spans the width of Malaspina, the lagoon's half-mile circle is too small to notice. But it is the most likely thing to kill the glacier.

Along the rim of ice, drips hung from green moss curtains. Trees grew in the shapes of writhing snakes, bending toward the sun as the ground shifted beneath them. Following the shore, we paddled through a tangle of shattered wood and piles of rubble. Marooned on an iceberg, a lone live spruce stood in a patch of leafless willow, leaning as the melting berg shrank beneath it.

Hig picked up a rock at the base of one of the rubble piles. "Look, there are *barnacles* here! Dead ones."

"Is it really that salty?"

He dipped a hand in the water, bringing it to his mouth to taste the chilly drips. "No. Fresh."

"They must have bobbed up on an iceberg," Hig continued. "So there must actually be a lot of ocean water in here, just stratified down to the bottom. And it must be deep too. I wonder if we could catch a fish?"

I relished the sleuthing, reminded of why I was once a scientist, of the fun before the narrowing specialization. Sitkagi was the other place we remembered from four years ago. It drew us back with the utter bizarreness of ice-top forests, and with the weight of four years of speculation. If this was the fastest-changing place in a rapidly changing world, what might happen while we watched?

We measured the depth later—around 150 feet. But we never did catch a fish.

Our Sitkagi Lagoon campsite had begun with a glowing recommendation from Carl: "Well, this site is kind of exposed and kind of bear-y, but I think it's the best we're going to do right here."

"I didn't find anything else that's so good that we should scramble to get there right now," Hig responded. Our plan was to camp near the lagoon, and dusk made camping a rather immediate proposition.

I ended it all with classic procrastination: "We can scout a better site tomorrow." But when tomorrow came, we paddled the lagoon instead, inertia compounding with the reassuring numbers of a sat phone–delivered weather forecast.

Hig: "Well, the storm's not supposed to bring much of a wind."

Carl: "And we're already here."

Michael: "I'd rather not move right now."

Me: "Flooding issues don't seem too bad here."

On day three, I remembered why I never count on weather forecasts. With both hands, I gripped the shuddering paddle shaft that served as our tent pole, grounding it to earth while the wall behind me pounded my head with every gust. Michael stood on the other side of the tent in a similar position. We formed human shields between the nylon and the hot stove-pipe. Outside, Hig weighted the loose corner of the tent with an even larger log, piled on top of a series of smaller rocks and logs, then crawled in, belly on the mud, through the one tiny gap he'd left along the edge. He spent a few minutes steaming, the warmth of the stove enveloping him in the vapor rising from his sopping clothes. Until the next tie popped free.

The bouldery shore was spread smooth with a thick frosting of sea foam. Chunks tore free, streaking across the surface, vaulting over the logs, and smacking like bubbly snowballs into our cluster of storm-besieged tents. Sopping wet people wriggled in and out of the mud patch by the crawl-in spot, pummeled by the tent as they warmed. They held up our roof—subsidiary tent poles—until each one in turn had to run out to deal with his own tent catastrophe. The kids played with thread and headlamps in their own puffs of steaming breath, heedless of the chaos. Michael perched on the mud, nodding seriously into the sat phone, rattling off wind speeds and rain rates, gathering a very personal forecast from his colleagues in the weather service. How much longer would this last?

A few more hours.

Right on schedule, the wind died, and we all crept outside, battered and relieved, cracking dumb jokes about our collective failure of a campsite choice. The world smelled like salt and was decorated in fragile jiggling pieces of sea foam. Then we crawled back in, still in the exact same spot, and fell asleep to claps of thunder, flashes of distant lightening, and a shower of hail.

The next morning, I balanced on a slippery log, watching a foot-deep rush of water sweep across our recently abandoned camp. Wave after brown wave churned from the lagoon's former shore, rubbing out our footprints, stripping the last brown leaves from the willows, and floating the logs that had anchored our tents to the earth. The storm was past, but the storm surge had only just arrived. The giant waves it built had begun to roll in, raising the lagoon beyond the tide book's prediction—already one of the highest tides of the year. We retreated with great haste and no dignity, scrambling over a series of logs to throw all our gear into the forest.

At the mouth of the lagoon, the small tidal stream was gone. In its place was three hundred yards of pitched battle between ocean and lagoon, waged across a field of giant boulders, armed with a javelin forest of trees. We were as high as we could get and as low as we dared be, cowering from the waves that crashed to the very top of the beach. The air roared salt. Beneath the light gray sky, the ocean was a foam of churning white. We yelled back and forth to be heard, each sentence punctuated by the crash of a wave and the thundering clatter of rocks and logs pulled out behind it.

The tide poured water out of the lagoon. The surf launched it back in. A tangle of tattered but still-green trees drew a curving boundary, tumbling back and forth with each arriving wave. The tide dropped further, sending the logs streaming out between the boulders. They hit the rocks like battering rams, flipping vertically in the surf, before escaping the clutches of the lagoon to barrel down the shore. Man-sized logs vaulted into the air, dressed in coats of foamy spray.

We had asked for this storm. Back in the hazy memories of trip planning, Hig had waxed excited about October's high tides, scheming to put us at the lagoon at just that time. "What if there's a big storm with one of those tides? That could be awesome to see."

Just inland from the beach, we'd measured the lagoon at 150 feet deep. Just offshore, it dropped off equally steeply. To the east, a shallow stretch of ocean was revealed by a band of waves that broke across a mile of sea. But here at the lagoon mouth, nothing was shallow enough to touch them—until each arrived on shore with a crash that shook the ground. The beach we stood on was merely the tip of a tall and precarious ridge. Built of loose boulders, and cored in some places by melting ice, the shore at Sitkagi was the most poorly engineered seawall I could imagine. We wanted to see the storm because we knew it would be tested. Because we knew it would never be rebuilt. Because we wanted to feel the fragility of the glacier's last defense.

$\backsim$

We took pictures of our friends taking pictures, all of us relishing the orange glow of sunset on surf and icebergs—the calm that followed the storm. It was their last day with us, in a week spent mostly on the shores of this lagoon. I knew they didn't share our interest in the details of the geology, but who could fail to appreciate that power? That glimpse of gorgeous light?

"Well, they really nailed it with the light rain forecast," Carl noted sarcastically the next morning, dripping at the top of the beach. They were all headed out now, walking to meet the plane that would take them to another plane, on a preordained schedule based on numbers and dates. I wasn't sure if the timing was good or bad, or how any of them really felt about their part in our journey.

"It is light rain," Michael corrected, donning his official weather-forecaster persona. "It's less than one-tenth of an inch per hour."

"That's all it ever does here, for hours and hours and hours," Carl countered. "They should call it steady f***ing boatloads of rain."

Sam stayed quiet. And with that, it was just the four of us again.

It *was* awesome to see. At a lower tide, I climbed over freshly shattered logs, their ends bright-brown and newly broken. The rocks' green cloak of algae was pocked with gray, where colliding boulders had broken off head-sized chunks. A boulder as big as a refrigerator stood out oddly red among the green, covered with an algae that lived only in deeper water. The waves had carried the entire rock up the beach.

The storm brought awe in the drama of waves—and in the glimpse of the future. Boulders are difficult to erode, but here they were eroding, tumbling down the face of Sitkagi's fragile seawall. That one storm did more to erode the channel than a year of normal tides, sending more warm ocean water to chew at the lagoon's walls of ice. The map's Sitkagi Bluffs have become Sitkagi Lagoon, and they'll soon become Sitkagi Bay. The vast lobe of Malaspina Glacier sits on ground far below sea level. As the ice retreats, the sea will move in, repeating a sequence followed by most of the bays in coastal Alaska. Each storm widens the channel between Sitkagi Lagoon and the ocean. The wider channel carries larger icebergs, which erode the channel more, until waves can crash directly on cliffs of rapidly retreating ice. Until Malaspina Glacier itself is a bay.

No one much will care about the demise of Malaspina Glacier. It's in no one's view. Cruise ships don't visit its forest-cloaked edge—though they might, when it becomes a bay. And the bay it leaves behind will probably be as stunning as the postglacial fjords that line the Alaska coast today. That beautiful bay will be a piece of climate-change legacy we can feel proud to give our kids.

Even as all its melting ice erodes the rest of their shores.

Predictions from climate change models often focus on the year 2100. The temperature might rise by 2 degrees Celsius by then. Or 4.5 degrees Celsius. Or 6.5. Sea level could be forty or fifty-six inches higher. Much of that uncertainty is not science, but people—in how much more oil and coal we'll burn, how far we'll fill the air with carbon dioxide before pulling back from our own disaster.

In all of those year 2100 maps, Alaska is a brightly colored blotch at the far edges of the color range—bright red with dramatically higher temperatures, dark blue with greater precipitation, the ocean surrounding it blue as well with the disappearance of ice. None of the world is the color I grew up with. All of the lines marking temperature and sea level tilt inexorably upward as the years tick forward. And then the maps and graphs end. Which seems fine, at first. The year 2100 is impossibly far away, distant enough to be a theoretical curiosity.

But a quick mental subtraction tells me that in 2100, Lituya will be eighty-nine years old. One of her great-grandmothers lived longer than that. It's not just possible that she'll be alive then. It's actually reasonably likely. All the frightening up-sloped lines that end at 2100 don't actually end. The carbon dioxide in the atmosphere stays for hundreds of years. Its impacts keep going, raising temperatures for centuries and sea level for millennia. Any grandchildren I may have will almost certainly be alive beyond the end of those graphs. Beyond what even the climate scientists care to worry over. I bequeath to them the gorgeous fjords of Malaspina Bay. But what else will they live to see?

17: Discovery

KATMAI CAREFULLY ADDED another stick to his "fancy stack" of fire-wood, forming an impressively precarious tower. Hig stirred the noodles. I dug in the bottom of a dry bag for dried vegetables and spices. Lituya mouthed a water bottle top. Rain blew against the wall in a familiarly depressing clatter.

"I can't help thinking about our alternate selves who got in that plane yesterday with everyone else. Not that I *really* would have, but . . ." I gestured outside, leaving the difficulties of the day unspoken.

"We should have done this as a day hike," Hig chimed in. "I would have liked more time at Sitkagi Lagoon."

We had all the time in the world, and too many goals for every day of it. The days were growing short—nine hours from sunrise to sunset—and most of those hours passed by in the basic building blocks of expedition life. Getting firewood and water, cooking on our tiny stove, eating meals and snacks, changing diapers, charging batteries, fixing gear, setting up camp or breaking it down, inflating the packraft, and trekking to our next location. The real goals of our expedition—experiencing the wonders of this land-scape; documenting Malaspina's changes in pictures, words, and a handful

Hig's footprints in slushy snow on the edge of Malaspina Lake of numbers; introducing the kids to their own grand adventure—battled to fill the spaces that remained.

Hig took the pot off the stove and passed it to me, feeding the fire with one of the few sticks Katmai hadn't already co-opted as building blocks. I blew on a steaming mouthful. Curry, cheese, and noodles was one of my favorites.

~⁀~

We had actually scouted this route yesterday. Or Hig had. I had plopped down to nurse Lituya in the crevassed forest, while Katmai traced circles around us, discovering all the mosses on the ground.

"Spruce tree moss!"

"That's nice, Katmai. What else do you see?"

"Feather moss!" I didn't know the real names, but I could see the shapes in his inventions.

Hig crashed back to greet us in a breathless excitement, barely returning within the forty-five minutes he'd promised. "I really think we should go that way tomorrow." He offered to tell me everything he'd seen, but thought it would make an amazing surprise. I preferred the coast—more beautiful and straightforward, and not short on interest or upheaval of its own. Think of that storm! But I couldn't quite resist Hig's enthusiasm. Or his promised surprise. So the next day, we followed the lagoon's icy cliffs back toward the bulk of the glacier.

"It's a few short sections of raft-carrying between paddling stretches, and then we're almost at the ice lake," Hig pronounced as we set off.

~⁀~

Wrist-thick branches of dead alder crisscrossed around my legs, obscuring my feet where they perched on another pair of dead alder branches. Beneath those were more dead branches, piled in a rotten tangle stretching down to somewhere about ten feet beneath me, where, in a rare gap between the twigs, I could see the bottom of the crevasse. Dead alder branches are not very strong.

But there was nowhere to fall to, and I had nothing else to step on, so I gingerly poked my foot ahead until I was standing at the base of a vertical slope of ice, melted slick in the sun. On my back, Lituya slept, as heedless of this difficulty as she was of every other. Ten feet above me, Hig and Katmai chattered with unreasonable cheer, both enjoying the jungle-gym of live alder on top of the ice. My feet flailed in the slick mud of a V-shaped notch, and I grabbed a trunk of alder as a chin-up bar, hauling myself up onto their slightly flatter ground.

"I think this is a contender for the worst bushwhack ever!" Hig crowed, grinning.

The entire route was only a few hundred yards—and took a full day to navigate. It was bad enough to be funny, even in the moment. We did eventually reach Hig's amazing surprise. It was a maze of peninsulas and islands. It was a glacial trash pile of rubble-sharp rocks, drifts of old wood, upside-down bushes, and shattered trees. It was a stairway of car-sized ice blocks, running up to the toppling forest above. It was a sheer cliff of vertical gray ice, striped with horizontal bands of darker gray, throwing ice boulders into the water beneath it. Camped nearby, we heard the crashing roar of one of those calvings. I had become enough of a connoisseur of forests-on-ice to enjoy a stunningly dramatic example of the form.

⌒⌒

It wouldn't be here long. Despite the many hours it had taken us to traverse the crevasse maze, only two narrow ice walls separated this lake from Sitkagi Lagoon—one about thirty feet wide, the other about twenty. They looked even more precarious than the narrow spine of boulders that guarded the lagoon's seaward shore. Soon (Hig thought within a few years) the last of the ice walls would crumble, more than tripling the size of the lagoon, pulling in more ocean with every tide, and taking one more step toward the disintegration of the ice.

Melting ice expands the lagoon, which melts more ice, which expands the lagoon. It was one small example of a positive feedback loop. Positive only in name, climate change is full of these vicious circles—amplifying and accelerating the warming we've already started. Melting Arctic permafrost sends trapped methane—a greenhouse gas more potent than carbon dioxide—into the atmosphere, where it warms the air to melt more permafrost. In the Arctic Ocean, sea ice melts to reveal dark-colored water, which absorbs more sunlight than ice, heating up. Darker warmer water melts more ice around it, amplifying the pattern. The same pattern happens on land. Trees now grow where shrubs were before, and shrubs spread into former tundra. Their dark branches stick above the winter snow, absorbing sunlight, warming and melting the snow from dark needles and black twigs, continuing the cycle of warming.

There are more such circles. The warming humans have started feeds back on itself, amplifying our problems.

We returned to the coast to find the dead sea lion gone from Dead Sea Lion Stream. So were the logs. Much of the sand. Even the stream itself wasn't in quite the same place. Spruce roots trailed down a steep sand bluff, across a gap of missing dirt. Their ends tangled with piles of washed-up kelp at the top of the beach—forest abruptly meeting ocean. On the more exposed stretches of shore, the storm we'd watched at Sitkagi had tossed dead fish into forest moss and mushrooms, while snapping tree trunks onto the gravel below.

According to Michael's estimate, the winds were only about fifty miles an hour. The waves they brought eroded ten feet of forest floor. This happens all the time. Along parts of this coast, the erosion reaches fifty feet a year. It happens because the glacier is melting, taking the beaches along with it in another vicious circle. Lakes form at the edge of the melting ice, swallowing all the glacier's sand and gravel before it can reach the beach. Without that sediment to protect and rebuild it, the ocean eats the shore away.

The erosion here is specific to the peculiarities of a glacier-fed coast. And general to the world. Climate change brings sea level rise. The maps of these future oceans are often drawn with a simple blue line, contouring the shore as if sea level rise were nothing more than the filling of a bathtub. As if anyone sitting above that blue line has nothing to worry about. But coastlines are controlled by a balance of sand. A few inches of water would bury offshore sand flats, pushing them out of equilibrium with the ocean. To regain that balance, more sand must flow in, replacing the drowned beaches by eroding the coasts above them. People who live on soft bluffs perched above the ocean, like many in Cook Inlet and Puget Sound, are as threatened as those who live at sea level.

One of the paradoxes of being out here was that I wanted to see the ice fail. Climate change is a global tragedy. The scientific models get gloomier and gloomier with every iteration, as ever-faster warming easily outpaces our meager attempts to bring it in check. I can easily rattle off a depressing list of the impacts already being felt, by humans and nonhumans alike. I've *seen* them. We, and especially our kids, are on track to live through even more catastrophic shifts, both ecologic and economic. I know all that. I care about it. I worry over the climate impacts of minor personal decisions, and the major decisions of governments. But my allegiances had temporarily shifted. Here, it was hard not to root for climate change.

Violent transformation is frightening. But it's also exciting. Disasters captivate and enthrall us, drawing on the primal impulse that brings us to rubberneck at car crashes, and glue our eyes to the world's televised tragedies. One of Hig's favorite childhood books was a litany of earthquakes and floods titled *Great Disasters*. He spent his graduate school years chasing the aftermath of the globe's tsunamis. But disaster captured me too, and probably all of us. In my journal, the words I kept coming back to over and over again were: "a world transformed."

The one thing our kids were sure to inherit was something different than our status quo. Depending on how it all works out, we might live to see a good bit of the transformed world ourselves. Objectively, it was hard not to imagine their future as more difficult than our own. But I had to hope there might be some good hiding in that catastrophe. Some positives that come from waking up to all of our failures: beauty created in the inevitable overhaul.

Sometimes it seemed like we spent a lot of time seeing nothing at all. We had two headlamps. And then we had one headlamp. And now we had one headlamp that shone only with an extremely dim strobe-like flickering, just enough to light up a few lines on a page from a few inches away. That one was off now, its remaining power carefully rationed. The cracks of orange light around the stove door barely illuminated Hig's face. Lituya and Katmai were only cheerful silhouettes, wildly tossing mittens and socks they couldn't see. The ideal of "solar power" had run up against the reality that was "Alaska November."

November hadn't brought us any weather with the drama of the Sitkagi storm. But it was bringing more and more days like this one—short gray days between long black nights, both spent beneath confining walls, listening to the mournful rhythm of drumming rain turning to hissing snow turning to rain then snow again.

Katmai sat on the bed, building "airplanes" from shavings of wood and scraps of nylon, and performed elaborate rituals with the cones and buds of spindly alders that poked up within the tent. "You think it should be fall, but the weather thinks it should be winter!" he pronounced happily. Lituya fiddled with the cap of a water bottle, trying over and over again to put it on. I wished I remembered how to play. Then they both fell asleep in my lap. In every sense of the word, I was stuck.

"You know what I miss?" I grumbled to Hig. "Chairs."

He laughed.

"No really, I mean it. It's been a month and a half since we've been indoors anywhere, and I miss chairs more than anything. Chairs give you a measure of physical personal space that's kind of impossible here. Chairs mean you can't be climbed on so easily." I missed the chance to be, if only for an hour, out of reach of four grabbing hands, no longer a jungle gym, and able to finish one entire thought without picking up and relocating a child (usually Lituya, as she headed to destroy herself or some critical object).

"Well, they always say the thing about hitting your head on the wall is that it feels so good when you stop," Hig joked. "And I think there's some truth to that. Maybe discomfort like this makes you appreciate all the conveniences and comforts of your ordinary life."

You can tell the mood of a trip by whether the discussions tend toward the future or the past. By whether we spend our hours speculating with great excitement about what we might see next and daydreaming about future expeditions, or second-guessing everything from the trip design and gear choices to the exact location of our latest campsite.

I had never believed in the whole "man versus nature" thing. Most of the challenges of the wilderness seem more appropriately cast as "man's wise choices versus man's stupid ideas and unrealistic assumptions." Or woman's, I guess. I just wasn't sure on which side of that line to place a journey that extended through to mid-November. In our pretrip visions, we'd imagined this late-fall window would bring us fewer bears (no, still plenty of them around), amazing storms (yes, although this was seeming less and less like a recommendation), no crevasse-obscuring snow on the glacier (probably also true in August), gorgeous low-angle light (when there was light at all), and time to finish all our summer's harvest and gathering at the yurt before we set out (our stuffed-full chest freezer seemed less relevant while eating potato chips hundreds of miles away). There's always a price to pay for awesome experiences, but lately the ratio of oh-my-god-I-can't-believe-we're-in-such-an-amazing-place to I'm-huddling-in-the-tent-feeling-oppressed-by-blowing-sleet had been trending significantly downward.

The blessing and curse of the sat phone is that we never had to keep going. We could call the pilot any time and get picked up in the next gap of good weather on the next landable beach. That's exactly what we were planning to do in another ten days anyway. Who would ever know the difference? Retreat wasn't unmentionable, but even as our conversations lighted on that possibility, I never really considered it. I clung to stubbornness. Clung to my goal. We said we were going to spend two months out here and go to Malaspina Lake, and that's simply *what we were going to do*. I didn't want to fail, and I didn't want to admit that I had failed.

But mostly I still felt optimism. Not a simple optimism that the sun would be out tomorrow, or that our children would suddenly learn to carry a load. I clung to our plan because I believed, despite any immediate evidence to the contrary, that there were wonders left to behold even in this last edge of the glacier—wonders I couldn't yet imagine. That weather always changed. That there were discoveries to be made and rewards to be had, and I would miss this unknowable future more than I ever missed chairs and lights.

∽⌒∽

The tide pushed inland, reversing the flow of Sudden Stream, carrying our packraft all the way to the shore of Malaspina Lake. These names really were on the map, and I wondered what, a hundred years ago, had made the stream seem so *sudden*. We walked the shore, watching fog paint the lake an eerie gold-gray. The only ripples were the round heads of harbor seals, noiselessly popping up to ponder us before slipping back into the chilly water. Rocky islands hung in a misty confusion, water indistinguishable from the sky. The kids, asleep on our backs, added only peaceful breathing to the silence.

We had arrived. Our stretch of low morale had been broken a few days earlier, with the glimpse of a rainbow, the lightening color of raincoats drying on our shoulders, and air warm enough to send Katmai happily running down the beach to feed every one of the driftwood "dinosaurs." At Malaspina Lake, we circled back to amazement.

I was happy. With an undercurrent of pride, feeling that I'd been vindicated in my stubbornness, and relief at what we had to show our next guest, due to arrive tomorrow. Our friend Greg was planning to spend the last five days of the journey with us. He was a filmmaker. It would be easy to show Greg's camera a scene of cold and hardship to make viewers happy for their own cozy comforts. But I wanted to show them something that would make them sorry they *weren't* here.

∽⌒∽

"Um, there are some *very* fresh bear tracks right here."

I opened my eyes to the crisscrossing shadows of alders in moonlight, and Hig's head, poking through the tent door with his announcement. In the new snow, any track couldn't be more than an hour or two old.

"I'm going to go wake up Greg. Maybe give him our extra pepper spray."

In the still night, I listened for the telltale rhythmic click of our electric bear fence. My ears were sharpened by fear—by visions of those sharp claws, rippling muscles, and bone-cracking jaws circling our tent in the middle of the night. The fence was ticking now, but that didn't mean much. Something, most probably the incessant wetness of the last two months, had set it on the fritz, and it rarely worked for more than a few hours without needing its batteries to be reinserted. By now, the hour it took to tie all the crinkled strands of fishing line that held the electrified wire to the branches was more a matter of due diligence than actual protection. I slept anyway.

In the glow of the first clear dawn we'd had in weeks, my nervousness quickly faded to an ironic curiosity. Now that winter had come in earnest, why were we seeing more bear signs than ever? Golden light streamed across the snow, crunchy in the cold of a cloudless sky, the line of smallish bear tracks as hard as cement. The bear had circled the same tiny island we were camped on. Which was so tiny that we hoped no bears would have reason to come here, and so tiny that any bear that did was only a stone's throw from the tent. It had dug and eaten lupine roots, scattering dark gravel across the snow before disappearing into the water. The tracks showed no sign of curiosity about our presence, and no sign of fear.

Two days later, our tracks and the bears' were layered in a series of gently curving lines, footsteps on footsteps, some just faint impressions on a hard-frozen crust, some sinking deep when the snow had been slushy. I picked out the first bear, beneath a line of Hig's tracks from a run for fire-wood, then all of our tracks returning to camp the night before, and finally the wide swath of a packraft being towed as a sled . . . almost missing the latest set of paw prints in the built-up jumble.

"Hey Greg, I think this set here is new since last night," I said, point-ing with a mittened thumb. Hig and Katmai were already well ahead of us, throwing snowballs into the bear tracks on the delta.

"Really?" he asked a little nervously. "Okay, then," he continued more brightly, fiddling with the buttons of his video camera. "Could you say that again? Like you just saw them?"

That first night, waking Greg up with the "Um, just so you know, there's a bear right here next to where you're sleeping" had seemed a little cruel—an unnecessarily harsh punch line to a cold and exhausting day spent packrafting in the blowing sleet. I had been worried we wouldn't be able to show him enough fun. He was worried there wouldn't be enough photogenic oppression.

∽

"I need a barefoot crossing here!" Greg mock-pleaded. His tone was a deliberate caricature of a pushy director. But he really did want us to do it. The stream was a few feet wide, ankle deep, partially frozen, and surrounded on all sides by snow.

"Nope. Looks cold," Hig answered.

"Come on! After all I've seen, I can't believe *you guys* are complaining about cold feet."

"Why don't *you* cross barefoot then," I countered. "I'll hold the camera."

"It's not the same if I do it. And that was such a great scene in the first movie." Greg had put together the movie on our four-thousand-mile journey, from our own scattered pieces of footage. Fresh from his tour of the film festivals, he was eager to replicate that success.

"It's very rare that crossing barefoot actually makes sense. That time it was below freezing and our feet were actually dry," Hig pointed out.

"But the viewers won't know the difference."

I laughed, and kept walking. "No way."

Out on the abandoned river delta, we followed the tracks of a mom and two cubs where they had briefly followed our tracks from the day before. Further on, the small diamond prints of a fox wavered from their own trail to investigate ours. Then the fur-blurred steps of a wolverine.

Burdened with gear and kids, we usually set up base camps simply to avoid moving every single thing on every single day. But that gave us the freedom to circle back on ourselves. This was the first trip we could follow not just the tracks of other animals, but those of other animals tracking us.

∽

We were following the ghost of a river. Our satellite photos, four years old, showed it plainly. Now the rushing glacial river that poured into Malaspina Lake, that had carved out this valley and piled up sand to form a miles-wide delta, was gone.

The ice still melted. Water still flowed. But we didn't find the river until we were miles from where we'd expected, where silt-choked water flowed between cabin-sized blocks of ice. Then it slipped beneath a cliff, hollowing out a tunnel under the glacier as it disappeared in an echoing rush. The sculpted ice of the tunnel's roof glowed blue at the entrance, dark and mysterious against the veil of snow falling outside. Inside, the gentle sounds of dripping water were drowned out by the roar of the river boring into the hill. Katmai ran his hands over the slick wet cups and ribs of the cave wall. Deep in the tunnel the flow slowed, and Hig paddled the river as far as he dared. All I could see was the glow of his headlamp, like a lost spirit rising out of the darkness.

We had two days remaining now. One to paddle back to the coast, and one to catch the plane. This ice cave was the last new thing we would see. It was beautiful, its exquisite forms heightened by the fact that the cave was our own discovery. We were the first people to ever set foot here. Greg was the first person to ever reach the cave. Lituya was the youngest. Hig went farther into its depths than any other human.

It was exciting for exactly the opposite reason that most "firsts" are exciting. Most firsts represent a triumph of humankind, where some intrepid adventurer manages to scale a high peak or paddle a raging river that no human has ever managed before. This one had nothing to do with us. Entering this ice cave was a trivial effort, in a place where no one else happened to be. We were first here, because this world is re-created every year. Malaspina was melting so quickly that its edges were tenuous, inconsistent even from one year to the next. We couldn't predict where this river—now tunneling into the hill—might be in another few years, or where the edge of the lake would be, or how much ocean water would rush into it with every rising tide. We were the first people to visit the cave, and we might well be the last.

People can't stop Malaspina from melting. It takes decades for global temperature to catch up to carbon dioxide levels. It takes even more time for melting ice to catch up to temperature. We've decided its fate already. And we're deciding the fates of more and more places every day. Climate change solutions are often phrased in percentages and reductions—how much less carbon dioxide we're planning to emit in some future year than this year. But sooner or later, those emissions need to be basically zero. Not just to stabilize carbon dioxide concentrations at a relatively "safe" level, but to stabilize them at any level at all. "Sooner" is now. "Later" is only a few decades from now, and is a choice to stop burning fossil fuels nearly cold turkey, with all the economic hardship that implies. "Never" means temperature will never stabilize at all, plunging future generations into a series of endless catastrophes.

I spent years as a scientist. Hig works as a scientist, with scientists, every year. Scientists are a species known for pulling arguments apart from every possible angle, for a communication style full of probabilities and caveats and "but we can't rule out" statements, for waiting for evidence and shunning any overly hasty calls to action. Yet climate scientists are more worried about the future of climate change than anyone else. They see terrifying possibilities in obscure trends in Arctic sea ice, methane trapped beneath the Atlantic, and patches of ice exposed along permafrost coastlines—because they understand how these things connect to all of us. In this one issue, the scientists have become the shrillest "extremists" among us. That should tell us something.

Stabilizing those numbers matters. Whether we meet our carbon dioxide targets or miss them entirely, every degree makes a difference. Katmai and Lituya will grow up in a climate more difficult than today's. But humans can be resilient through difficult times. How much worse it will be still matters—and is up to us.

◦⁄◦

"I'm bushwhacking again! I like bushwhacking! Watch me bushwhack again!" Still wearing his life vest from the river crossing, Katmai barreled into every spindly alder sticking out of the snow, as we left the ice cave behind us. Out of time, Hig swept the boy onto his shoulders, and we turned back, following our snaking lines of tracks one last time as dusk crept across the snow, beneath an ominous red-gray sky. Holding the paddle, Greg towed our packraft as a sled, looking like a lost fisherman in rubber boots and heavy rubber raingear. Lituya was awake this time, smiling over my shoulder.

They'd never understand this journey, as much as they loved it. They'd never remember the two months where both Mom and Dad were around at every moment of the day, available for every exploration. But the ice, the bear tracks, the storms, the pebbles, the noodles and chocolate in the tent, and the silly dinosaur games on the beach—it would all become part of them.

We weren't home yet (or even at the pickup spot), but I was already feeling nostalgic. This whole journey had been a first. Our first trip with Lituya. Our first multiday glacier crossing. Our first trip with a heated tent. Our first trip with time and space to explore an area so deeply. And even as it was the first, it was also the last. The last time we will be able to carry all our gear and both our children. The last time we'll all fit in one packraft. The last time Katmai will be small enough to be worn beneath his father's coat, snuggling up warm against the snow.

How far would a three- or four-year-old be able to walk? Did I have enough hands to corral a more mobile Lituya in a packraft by myself while simultaneously paddling? No matter how much we do, we can never be experts. Children change as quickly as glaciers. Adventuring with kids is working incredibly hard to plan for something you can't possibly anticipate. Then adapting everything you know on the fly. Then throwing out every one of those techniques to start over from scratch the next time.

Despite all that, we do it anyway.

EPILOGUE
Around the Sun

JANUARY

My new red bicycle, with its studded ice tires and double-kid trailer, was gone. The snow had stolen it again, leaving not even a speck of handlebar showing above the drift. It didn't matter this morning. The bike's tires couldn't have gripped in the fresh dust and half-crushed snow that remained on the road.

At forty-nine pounds between them, I couldn't carry both kids on my body anymore. But I was still holding out against the specter of motorized transportation. Katmai climbed into the utility sled, his pale face barely visible in the tunnel of dark fur that ringed the hood of his parka, hands tucked deeply into its long sleeves. It was a miniature whaler's parka, handmade with a wolverine fur ruff—a gift from Point Hope. In addition to the parka, he was wearing pants, snow pants, a shirt, a fleece hoodie, two pairs of socks, and neoprene booties. Lituya was wearing a diaper, shirt, pants, fleece hoodie, booties, and a snowsuit, wrapped on my back beneath my raincoat, over my puffy jacket, sweater, and shirt, and above my pants, snow pants and gaiters. Between putting every one of those pieces on the appropriate set of limbs and navigating the hundred yards of snow-drifted trail between

Katmai walks a cobble beach on the coast near Malaspina Glacier.

us and the sled, I had been at it for an hour already. Getting to town would take another hour again.

But that didn't matter. Hig was out of town, and as much as we were out to do our errands, we were out to escape the confines of the yurt and the company of three. To enjoy the feet and feet of snow. I snapped a few pictures, posting them online with an offer of FREE SNOW for anyone in the Lower 48 who might be missing theirs. That year was a colder-than-average winter in Alaska, with record-breaking snows around the state. But in most of the country, it was bare brown and record-setting warm, with summer arriving months ahead of schedule and the warmest March in history.

Winters are as unique as the snowflakes they fail to bring. Next year might be different, but the trend is clear. I'm writing this on the 332nd consecutive month with global temperatures above the twentieth-century average. The last time the world was colder than usual, I was only five years old.

⌒

JUNE

My garden beds were shrouded in gauzy white row cover—lumpy ghosts. The sun hung high above the western mountains, guest of honor at our annual summer solstice party. The summer's first mosquitoes had showed up too, fat and slow and growing more numerous with the evening. Dozens of people trickled in and out, loading the table with bowls and pans. Dogs roamed for scraps and eyed the wobbling plates of toddlers. Children ran screaming through the woods.

"Would you mind if I peeked at your garden?" the postmistress asked.

"Of course! Here, let's just step in here and I'll show you around." I was thrilled that she'd asked. My huge bowl of just-picked salad shared space on the table with the rest of the potluck food, but I couldn't exactly go around crowing about how all of it had come from *my garden*. In June!

Katmai had been pulling and gobbling plump red radishes when many people were just starting to plant. I was bursting with that success. But I wasn't quite sure what I was proud of. That I'd been out here in April, shoveling snow off the edges of every bed to speed up the melt? That I'd followed tips from other local gardeners? Filled a smudged notebook with careful records of all my experiments? Lucked into a sunny swath of west-facing dirt?

"That's amazing! I can't believe how big your cabbages are already!"

I shrugged. "I was just really impatient this year and shoveled some snow, so that's why I planted so early . . . See, look over here, where the carrots are all shorter than on the other side of the bed. I didn't put enough compost in that soil. And I planted my cabbages too close together again. . . I've only been doing this a few years, so all this," I waved my hand across the garden, "is mostly just a few key tips I've picked up from some people. You could do it next year." It really was just a few key tips: buried carcasses of filleted-out salmon and kelp for fertility, raised beds and floating row cover for warmth, planted with quick-growing varieties that like the cool. I passed them on.

I passed the veggies on also, pressing plastic bags full of greens into the hands of departing guests. That was the success I really wanted. Having enough to be easily generous. To pass on something useful that everyone around me didn't already have. To give back.

⌒⌒

JULY

"Okay, now you have to run ahead and hide, but very, very far, and then I'll run to you and you take a picture of me when I get there!" Katmai told Hig.

Hig took off in a goofy exaggerated run, disappearing around the corner.

"It's time to go!" Katmai yelled, his rubber boots slapping on the hard dirt trail as he chased his disappearing dad. I followed, cringing a little that we hadn't yet found him any real hiking shoes.

"Mai-mai running and running! Daddy hiding! My down! My running also!" Lituya piped up from over my shoulder, wriggling in the wrap in her excitement to join her brother.

Katmai sprinted up to where Hig lay, belly on the muddy trail, nearly colliding with him in a fit of giggles. Lituya was one and a half years old now, stretched out from a baby into a bundle of toddler energy desperate to catch up to her big brother. Katmai was three-and-a-half.

He thought this was a game. We knew it was a training regimen. Our grand plan began taking shape in November's snow and rain, as we brainstormed designs for packable, beach-capable carts and wagons while struggling down Malaspina's beaches without them. We circled Alaska in our minds, looking for the next idea big enough to excite us beyond considerations of snow and rain and wilderness diapering. Half a year later, it seemed we had finally passed beyond the low point for mobility with kids. The ever-increasing weight of our children (fifty-two pounds now) was finally outweighed by their ability to transport themselves.

Expeditions are how Hig and I frame our lives. I feel naked without those plans—never quite comfortable until we schedule the next adventure. A few months after Katmai turns four and Lituya turns two, we plan to packraft and walk around Cook Inlet. The eight hundred miles might take us four months, or three, or even five. But this time, Katmai will be hiking on his own two feet.

Why Cook Inlet? Cook Inlet is the heart of modern Alaska. It has Native villages and Russian villages, hippie towns and industrial camps, and Anchorage, Alaska's biggest city. It has Seldovia. It has oil rigs and natural gas plants, coal mine proposals and tidal power proposals, endangered whales and abundant bears, salmon and melting glaciers. It has most of Alaska's population, and hundreds of miles of nearly unpeopled wilderness.

The future of Malaspina Glacier is clear. The future of Cook Inlet is muddier and more conflicted, and maybe more important. It's a place where all the diverse issues of Alaska's future collide with the diversity of all its people. Where we can ask them what they think.

About the Author

ERIN MCKITTRICK grew up in Seattle, exploring the wilderness of the
nearby Cascade Mountains. She met her husband, Hig, at Carleton College,
where she graduated with a BA in biology in 2001. Erin also has a master's
degree in molecular and cellular biology from the University of Washington.
After college, Erin and Hig took off on their first major Alaska adventure
together, setting them both on a new life path.

Erin is the author of *A Long Trek Home: 4,000 Miles by Boot, Raft,
and Ski*. Her writing also appears in *National Parks Magazine, Wend,* and
a number of online outlets. In addition to writing, she works for an environmental consulting firm and helps run a nonprofit organization, Ground
Truth Trekking. Ground Truth Trekking combines the "ground truth" of
wilderness expeditions with the "researched truth" of science, to shed light
on the crucial natural resource issues facing Alaska and the world. Learn
more at www.GroundTruthTrekking.org.

Erin lives with her husband and two children in Seldovia, Alaska, a
400-person fishing village unconnected to the road system.

recreation • lifestyle • conservation

MOUNTAINEERS BOOKS, including its two imprints, Skipstone and Braided River, is a leading publisher of quality outdoor recreation, sustainability, and conservation titles. As a 501(c)(3) nonprofit, we are committed to supporting the environmental and educational goals of our organization by providing expert information on human-powered adventure, sustainable practices at home and on the trail, and preservation of wilderness.

Our publications are made possible through the generosity of donors, and through sales of more than 500 titles on outdoor recreation, sustainable lifestyle, and conservation. To donate, purchase books, or learn more, visit us online:

MOUNTAINEERS
BOOKS

Mountaineers Books
1001 SW Klickitat Way, Suite 201
Seattle, WA 98134
800-553-4453
mbooks@mountaineersbooks.org
www.mountaineersbooks.org